FIELD DEPENDENCE IN PSYCHOLOGICAL THEORY, RESEARCH, AND APPLICATION

FIELD DEPENDENCE
in
PSYCHOLOGICAL THEORY, RESEARCH, AND APPLICATION

Two Symposia in Memory of Herman A. Witkin

Edited by

Mario Bertini
Luigi Pizzamiglio
University of Rome

Seymour Wapner
Clark University

LEA LAWRENCE ERLBAUM ASSOCIATES, PUBLISHERS
1986   Hillsdale, New Jersey   London

Lawrence Erlbaum Associates, Inc., Publishers
365 Broadway
Hillsdale, New Jersey 07642

Library of Congress Cataloging in Publication Data

Main entry under title:

Field dependence in psychological theory, research and
  application.

  "One symposium, 'Style in cognition and culture,' was
organized by Seymour Wapner and took place in the
Eastern Psychological Association Meetings in Hartford,
Connecticut, U.S.A., on April 11, 1980. ... The second
symposium, 'La Dipendenza dal campo,' was organized by
Mario Bertini and Luigi Pizzamiglio and took place at
the Institute of Psychology, University of Rome, Italy
on November 28-29, 1980" — Pref.
  Bibliography: p.
  Includes indexes.
  1. Field dependence (Psychology) — Congresses.
I. Witkin, Herman A. — Congresses. I. Witkin, Herman A.
II. Bertini, Mario. III. Pizzamiglio, Luigi. IV. Wapner,
Seymour, 1917–
BF323.F45F54   1985   150   85-4530
ISBN 0-89859-668-8

Printed in the United States of America
10 9 8 7 6 5 4 3 2 1

Contents

List of Contributors

Dr. Mario Bertini
Department of Psychology
University of Rome
Via Castro Pretorio #20
Rome, Italy 00185

Dr. Renzo Carli
Department of Psychology
University of Rome
Via Castro Pretorio #20
Rome, Italy 00185

Dr. Donald R. Goodenough
Graduate School of Education
Rutgers University
New Brunswick, NJ 08903

Dr. Sheldon J. Korchin
Department of Psychology
University of California
Berkeley, CA 94720

Dr. Franco Lancia
Vicolo Magisterna 1
Velletri, (Rome), Italy 00100

Dr. Helen Block Lewis
19 Chauncy Street
Cambridge, MA 02138

Dr. Samuel J. Messick
Educational Testing Services
Princeton, NJ 08540

Dr. Philip I. Oltman
96 Mason Drive
Princeton, NJ 08540

Dr. Rosa Maria Paniccia
Via Coronari 189
Rome, Italy 00100

Dr. Luigi Pizzamiglio
Department of Psychology
University of Rome
Via Castro Pretorio #20
Rome, Italy 00185

Dr. Evelyn Raskin
56 Seventh Avenue
New York, NY 10011

Dr. Seymour Wapner
Psychology Department
Clark University
950 Main Street
Worcester, MA 01610

Dr. Pierluigi Zoccolotti
Department of Psychology
University of Rome
Via Castro Pretorio #20
Rome, Italy 00185

Preface

This volume contains papers presented at two symposia in honor and memory of the late Herman A. Witkin. One symposium, "Style in Cognition and Culture," was organized by Seymour Wapner and took place at the Eastern Psychological Association Meetings in Hartford, Connecticut, April 11, 1980. It contained "Introductory Remarks" by Seymour Wapner; "History of the Field Dependence Construct," by Donald R. Goodenough; "Psychological Differentiation Theory in Social and Cross-Cultural Psychology," by Philip K. Oltman; "Clinical Implications of Field Dependence," by Helen Block Lewis; "Counseling Implications of Field-Dependence-Independence in an Educational Setting," by Evelyn Raskin; and "Herman Witkin and the Meaning of Style," by Samuel Messick.

The second symposium, "La Dipendenza dal Campo," was organized by Mario Bertini and Luigi Pizzamiglio and took place at the Institute of Psychology, University of Rome, Italy, November 28–29, 1980. It contained the following presentations: "Introductory Remarks," by Seymour Wapner; "History of the Field Dependence Construct," by Donald R. Goodenough; "Implications of Field Dependence for Social Psychology," by Renzo Carli, Franco Lancia and Rosa Maria Paniccia; "Some Implications of Witkin's Teaching for Sleep and Dreaming," by Mario Bertini; "Field Dependence, Personality Theory and Clinical Research," by Sheldon J. Korchin; "Individual Differences: Cerebral Structure and Cognitive Characteristics," by Luigi Pizzamiglio and Pierluigi Zoccolotti; and "Implications of Field Dependency for Education," by Mario Bertini.

In addition, at the symposium in Rome, there were a number of short research papers. These were "Witkin's Embedded Figures Test in Italian

Samples," by T. M. Fogliani Messina, A. M. Fogliani and S. DiNuovo; "Cognitive Differentiation and Integration in Aging," by C. Laicardi Pizzamiglio; "Prism Induced Tilts and Changed Felt Head Position," by R. B. Morant; "The Measurement of Field Articulation in German Preschool Children," by R. Schwarzer and C. Schwarzer; "Field Dependence-Independence: Toward an Animal Model," by P. Renzi and C. Violani; "Psychological Differentiation and Field Dependence as a Function of Early Interactions: A study in 32 Rural Children," by R. Gaddini De Benedetti; and "Muscle Tone and Cognitive Style," by V. Ruggieri. These research papers have been mainly published elsewhere and are not reprinted in this volume.

This book is symbolic of the affection and high regard in which Hy Witkin is held by colleagues and fellow scientists all over the world. It is concerned with the present and with the future. The powerful impact of Witkin's scholarly efforts on contemporary psychology is self-evident. The theoretical and research problems opened by his work shapes its potential for advancing the human sciences in the future and improving the lot of mankind.

We thank Dr. Donald Goodenough for his constructive comments and suggestions on an earlier version of the final chapter of this book. We also thank Maryjane Minor for her help in editing, typing and preparing the manuscript for publication.

Mario Bertini,
Luigi Pizzamiglio
Seymour Wapner

1 Introductory Remarks

Seymour Wapner
Clark University

Herman Witkin — distinguished scholar, colleague, friend — was born on August 2, 1916, and died on July 8, 1979, just a few weeks before his 63rd birthday. He was internationally known for his creative studies on cognitive style, first described as field dependence-independence and later integrated under the more general rubric of psychological differentiation. The pervasiveness of his impact on psychology and related fields, through his work on cognition and personality, derives from a number of sources. These include: A creative formulation and powerful attack on the problem of cognitive style at different levels of organization — biological, psychological, and sociocultural; a unique integration of the perspectives of psychoanalytic ego psychology; the psychology of individual differences and experimental cognitive psychology in the empirical and theoretical treatment of cognitive style; an integration of perceiving, thinking, and other psychological processes in a unified conception of the human being; and breadth in empirical investigations which encompass the clinical, developmental, educational, social, and cross-cultural domains of inquiry.

Each of us had close working relations with Hy Witkin. Each of us was a close friend. The remarkable thing is that many other people in this country and distant places had a similar relationship with this extraordinary, warm, modest human being. He had the special skill to make manifest the better, the warmer, the more creative hidden capacities of others. That this is so and will continue to be so for those he touched directly is self-evident; that it is true as well for those he touched indirectly through his writings is evident from the thousands of articles, papers, and books that have been stimulated by the work he initiated. In this book we shall speak about Hy in a way I believe he would have liked. We shall speak through the voices of a representative sample of his coworkers who will tell the broader profession about the range of ideas that grew from the exciting intellectual and human atmosphere which followed Hy wherever he went; ideas that developed and matured in places like Ingersoll Hall at Brooklyn College, in the halls of Downstate Medical School, at the Educational Testing Service, in England, in Italy, in Holland, in his living room, even during a walk in the woods. Here, we shall experience Hy Witkin's influence on psychology through the voices of his colleagues.

It is of special significance that two conferences in different parts of the world were presented honoring Herman A. Witkin. Having one conference in the United States and one in Rome speaks to the international impact of his work, to the international range of his collaborators, to the breadth and depth of his friendships, and to the impact of his seminal ideas on the psychology of the future.

The highly creative programs of research on cognitive style that was initiated by and conducted under Hy Witkin's leadership for almost four decades is very widely known. It continues to provide extraordinary stimulation to workers in a broad variety of fields on the international scene. This is evident from Witkin's high ranking among the 100 most cited psychologists in the 1975 Social Science Citation Index, and the inclusion of *Psychological Differentiation* as one of the 100 most frequently cited books.

Hy's collaboration with a spectrum of people from a variety of disciplines and interests tells us about him as a person, as well as the far reaching significance of his work. He was a true collaborator, interested in the ideas of others, and in sharpening his own views. He fostered synergistic relations with others. His curiosity, broad training, and interests — with a background ranging from comparative animal psychology (under the tutelage of Ted Schneirla) to psychoanalysis — made it natural for him to attack the problem of cognitive style at different levels of organization, i.e., the biological, the psychological, and the sociocultural.

Such all encompassing interests made for a remarkably broad range of people with whom he collaborated. At the biological level there was collaboration with Pizzamiglio in Rome and Oltman at The Educational Testing Service (ETS) on relations between field dependence-independence and brain organization. There is the work on behavioral genetics he conducted with an interdisciplinary group from Denmark, and other places, this group included Candini, Goodenough, Hirschhorn, Mednick, Owen, Schiavi, Schulzinger, and others.

At the psychological level, there was great diversity of collaboration including work on perception and psycho-physical underpinnings of field-dependence-independence with Goodenough at ETS; work on sleep and dreams with Bertini, of Rome; work on dreams, shame, guilt and psychopathology with Lewis, at Yale; work on communications including body language with Freedman, of State University of New York, Downstate Medical Center; work on doctor-patient relationships with Luborsky, of the University of Pennsylvania; work on education and career guidance with Raskin, of Brooklyn College, and collaboration with many other colleagues and students.

At the socio-cultural level of organization, there are the early studies on child rearing conducted with Ruth Dyk; the studies on social conformity with Price-Williams (UCLA) and other colleagues in Holland (Van Meel), in Italy (Bertini), Mexico (Ramirez), Norway (Christiansen); the extensive collaboration with Berry, including studies with mobile hunting and sedentary agricultural groups, studies on child-rearing practices of Pygmy hunting and Bantu agriculturists in the Central African Republic. There is the study on differential adaptability of people with different cognitive styles dependent on the environmental context that was to be conducted in India. There is the volume on the development of cognitive style in Africa where Hy was collaborating with co-workers from Canada (Berry), the Netherlands (van de Koppel), Scotland (Annis), France (Bahuchet) and Italy (Cavalli-Sforza). Such a listing of studies and collaborators as is being attempted here cannot be ventured without making special mention of those people at ETS—such as Goodenough, Oltman, and other scholars including Ehrlichman, Wiener, Sigman, Zoccolotti, Nowak, Moore and Rapaczynski—with whom Hy most recently had ongoing, day-to-day collaborative relationships involving work at all of these levels of organization and the relations among them.

This impressive list of extensive, yet integrated, studies and relationships with so many people not only points to the enormous range of Hy's interests and activities, but also tells more. One cannot have such relationships with colleagues without possessing special personal characteristics. Underpinning these personal, yet working, relationships were Hy's warmth, empathy, and understanding of others; his respect for the other's viewpoint coupled with commitment to his own; his openness to others; his maintenance of a network of close friendships through contact and correspondence; his concern, enthusiasm, and zest for people, for ideas, and for things around him.

My own thoughts date back to the early days at Brooklyn College, when an enthusiastic group of young scholars were tilting chairs, rotating rooms, disembedding figures, and making bets on what personality picture would accompany this or that pattern of scores on a battery of perceptual tests sampling field-dependence-independence. I have a vivid image of that day in Forest Hills, New York, when a number of us were joyous over Karen Machover's close to perfect blind predictions of perceptual performance from draw-a-person pictures spread over her living room floor. I recall those fantastic walks along the road near Hy's home in Princeton, walks that were interpenetrated by the quiet of the countryside on the one hand and by the state of the world on the other. I have a clear memory of silly talk mixed with serious talk, and of his devilish smile.

I think about the time the Witkins, the Bertinis and the Wapners met in Firenze. I recall with delight the fun in seeing Hy giggle over trapping me into eating fringuelli cooked on a spit, a delicacy that Mario Bertini had previously trapped Hy into ordering for himself.

Hy Witkin will continue to have impact on psychology because he himself satisfied his own criterion of the measure of a person's work. As Helen Lewis reports, Hy believed that the measure of a person's work is reflected in the ". . . questions one asks, the lines of inquiry [which] are opened up, . . . the extent to which one has stimulated others to answer questions which raise more questions" (Lewis, Chapter 6).

Hy's presence in the future scientific world will grow because of the legacy he has left us. It will sprout from the seeds that he planted in the powerful empirical, theoretical contributions he bequeathed to us and to future generations. For those fortunate enough to have known him personally, there was something special. We were changed, we were enriched. We shall continue to grow by having known him. And now I hear Hy's quiet voice asking, "Wapner! Hadn't we better now turn to substantive issues?"

2 History of the Field Dependence Construct

Donald R. Goodenough
Rutgers University

Those of us who worked with Hy Witkin over the years were aware of the many unique qualities that contributed to his genius. But even casual acquaintances were amazed by the range of his activities and interests. At the time of his death he was working with an international team on a cross-cultural study of Pygmy and Bantu people, in the Central African Republic of Zaire. He was working with another international team, in Denmark, on a study of sex chromosome anomalies. At the same time he was working at the Educational Testing Service in Princeton on a study of teaching and learning styles in the classroom, on a study of doctor-patient relationships in psychotherapy, and on a factor analytic study of individual differences in perceptual-cognitive functioning.

Even more amazing was Hy's ability to treat the concepts and findings from all these areas within a single, unifying theoretical framework. Each study was a facet in his overall research program on the nature and origins of individual differences in field dependence — a program that Hy began in 1941 with experiments on spatial orientation perception and that he continued throughout an historical period spanning almost forty years.

In the beginning, Hy was working in collaboration with Solomon Asch on laboratory studies that are now classics (Asch & Witkin, 1948a; 1948b; Witkin & Asch, 1948a; 1948b). The question was, How important are visual cues in perceiving the vertical direction of space? The strategy was to create a conflict between visual and gravitational cues. In the Rod-and-Frame Test, for example, the conflict was created by showing a tilted square frame in an otherwise dark room. The importance of visual cues in resolving the conflict was measured by asking subjects to adjust a rod to the vertical position.

The Rod-and-Frame Test is still commonly used, but it was not the only, or even the first, test developed for measuring a person's manner of conflict resolution. A tilting-room test, a rotating-room test, and many other ingenious devices were created for Hy's pioneering studies, and the term *field dependent* was first used to describe the effects of the tilted visual fields used in these tests.

The finding was that people differ dramatically in degree of field dependence, a finding that is now well known but that was unexpected at the time of discovery. We may recall that the sensory and perceptual experiments of the 1940s were commonly used on a few subjects, at most, and differences among normal people were commonly thought of as problems in method, as errors or noise to be avoided, if possible. The occurrence of individual differences might have led a lesser genius to reject the error-prone method. But they led Hy Witkin in a different direction.

Hy soon discovered that individual differences in the effects of visual cues are not merely errors of method. People showed remarkable self-consistency in degree of field dependence across many tests of orientation perception (Witkin et al., 1954). With this finding, field dependence achieved the status of a construct, referring to the cross-situational communality.

Initially the construct was interpreted as a perceptual resolution of the cue conflict. Field-dependent people simply relied more on visual cues and less on body cues in resolving the conflict than did field-*in*dependent people. But the theory of field dependence was, for Hy, an ever-changing framework, continuously incorporating new discoveries and new insights about the nature of the dimension.

Perhaps the most startling discovery came when Hy found himself predicting, with some accuracy, how field dependent his subjects would be on the basis of brief conversations with them. Personality was evidently related somehow to manner of perceiving the upright in space.

With the hindsight that comes from 40 years of subsequent research, we know that the personality differences Hy saw are salient enough for almost anyone to see. For example, even casual conversations between strangers run a different course if the partners are matched in degree of field dependence than if the partners are mismatched in degree of field dependence (Witkin & Goodenough, 1977). But the 1940 theories of orientation perception provided no basis for expecting, and no way of understanding, a personality-perception relationship. Indeed, a lesser genius might have viewed conversations with subjects simply as a pleasant interlude in the laboratory routine, irrelevant to the research problem. But the conversations Hy Witkin had with his subjects were viewed in a different way.

Beginning with this early discovery, Hy became a leader of the New Look movement in perception of the 1940s, criticizing approaches to perceptual theory that were traditional at that time because they neglected the personality of the perceiver. In the New Look tradition, the question became, Where is the perceiver in field dependence theory? The answer was that personality may be expressed in perception even in the simplest of laboratory tests. His early work on this question is summarized in the landmark book *Personality Through Perception,* co-authored by Si Wapner (Witkin et al., 1954).

Among the many personality correlates of field dependence reported in the literature, those that involve social-interpersonal behavior played the largest role in the subsequent development of Hy's theory. It was clear from his early work that field-dependent subjects rely on other people to a greater extent than do field-independent subjects (Witkin, Dyk, Faterson, Goodenough, & Karp, 1962). By 1977, in his most recent review of the socio-interpersonal correlates of field dependence, Hy could draw on literally hundreds of studies in the literature to refine and extend his earlier views (Witkin & Goodenough, 1977). It became increasingly clear that field-dependent people are more socially oriented, as shown, for example, by greater attentiveness to interpersonal cues, by a preference for being physically close to people and by a greater emotional openness in communication with others. In contrast, field-independent people have a more abstract, impersonal orientation. They are not usually very interested in others, and they show greater physical and emotional distancing. In sum, field-independent people seem to function with a greater degree of individual autonomy in their social-interpersonal behavior.

Another important early discovery was Hy's finding that field independence in upright perception is related to success in locating camouflaged or embedded figures (Witkin et al., 1954). It led to a new interpretation of the field dependence construct and provided a new and much more convenient assessment method.

From a theoretical point of view, correlations with the Embedded-Figures Test seemed most parsimoniously understood in terms of a common require-ment for perceptual analysis. In this view, observers must disembed the rod from the surrounding frame in the Rod-and-Frame Test, for example; as they must similarly disembed the simple figure from the complex pattern in the Embedded-Figures Test. The disembedding interpretation was a major con-ceptual extension in the attempt to understand individual differences in up-right perception. Hy did not abandon his cue conflict theory of these differ-ences, but he thought of them now in terms of a cognitive capacity to disembed the rod or the body from the context provided by the visual field. By 1962, field independence had been redefined as the capacity to overcome, or analyze, an embedding context in perceptual functioning (Witkin et al., 1962).

This redefinition had an important consequence, in turn, from a practical point of view. Individual and even group administered versions of the Embedded-Figures Test became readily available and economical tools for use in measuring field dependence. Once the Embedded-Figures Test became an acceptable replacement for the tests of upright perception, research on field dependence accelerated rapidly. As new findings poured in from around the world, the outline of an even broader conceptual structure began to take shape in Hy's thinking about the field dependence dimension.

Perhaps central to Hy's theoretical work was his constant search for unifying constructs to incorporate findings from different areas of psychological study. As the search continued and new correlates of field dependence were discovered, more and more general constructs were introduced to account for the data. For example, when evidence was found of relationships between field independence and organizing abilities in problem-solving tasks, another dimension, articulated versus global field approach, was introduced to describe the newly discovered communality. As evidence accumulated on the correlates of field dependence in personality functioning, the differentiation construct was introduced to describe the communality (Witkin et al., 1962; Witkin & Goodenough, 1981; Witkin, Goodenough, & Oltman, 1979).

The constructs that resulted from this strategy were arranged in a pyramidal structure, with the most general construct at the apex, and the most specific at the base. The differentiation construct has been located at the apex of the structure since its introduction in Hy's second landmark book *Psychological Differentiation* (1962). Degree of differentiation was considered to be a major formal property of an organismic system. A more differentiated system was said to be in a relatively heterogeneous state, with greater separation of activities from each other within the system, greater specialization of function, and greater self-nonself segregation involving clear boundaries between an inner core of attributes, feelings, needs, and the outer world.

In Hy's 1962 conception, field independence was a very specific construct. Defined as a disembedding ability in perception, it was located near the base of the pyramid. In this view, field dependence was an expression of a more global or undifferentiated mode of cognitive functioning, and field independence was an expression of a more articulated, or differentiated, mode. The personality characteristics that were correlated with the tests of field dependence were also viewed as expressions of degree of differentiation. For example, the sense of separate identity that characterized the social behavior of field-independent people was viewed as an expression of greater self–nonself differentiation.

But the 1962 conception was only one stage in the evolution of Hy's theory of field dependence and psychological differentiation. The more general constructs in the pyramidal structure generated hypotheses about other correlates of the field dependence dimension, and the growing network of data was used, in turn, to modify and expand the theoretical framework.

The area of cerebral lateralization provides one clear example of how research has been stimulated by differentiation theory (Witkin et al., 1979; Witkin & Goodenough, 1981). Although Hy introduced the differentiation construct to account for the personality correlates of field dependence, he thought of individual development toward greater differentiation in broad organismic terms, including biological as well as psychological processes. It seemed possible, for example, that increasing separation of psychological functions might be accompanied, in some cases, by increasing specialization of cortical structures in the control of these functions. In 1962, it was hard to see how this hypothesis could be tested, and the question remained until techniques for distinguishing between the functional roles of the left and right hemispheres were developed by other investigators. Given these developments, differentiation theory suggested the hypothesis that field independence is related to hemispheric specialization of function, an hypothesis that is currently an active focus of research interest.

The area of spatial orientation perception provides another clear example of the interaction between constructs and data in the development of Hy's theory of field dependence. The cue conflict and disembedding theories of upright perception stimulated intensive research efforts to describe the processes responsible for the field dependence phenomena in more specific terms. By the mid-1970s there was evidence to suggest that field dependence in orientation perception might be due to a visual driving of the vestibular system (Bischof, 1974).

It became increasingly clear that objectively upright viewers of a tilted display respond in many of the same ways as when the vestibular system is stimulated by tilting the head in the opposite direction. For example, when the head is tilted to the side, ocular countertorsion occurs in which the eyes roll in the opposite direction from the head and come to rest at a slightly less tilted position than the head with respect to the gravitational vertical. Among upright observers, a torsional response of the eyes also occurs in the direction of frame tilt in the Rod-and-Frame Test. In other words, the eyes roll slightly in the direction of the frame (Goodenough, Sigman, Oltman, Rosso, & Mertz, 1979; Hughes, 1973). The countertorsional response that occurs when the head is tilted in the dark is due almost entirely to vestibular stimulation. It seemed possible, therefore, that eye torsion in the Rod-and-Frame Test might be due to a visual-vestibular interaction. Moreover, Hughes found that individual differences in torsional amounts are related to individual differences in the rod-and-frame illusion. Visually induced torsion in the Rod-and-Frame Test is greater in field-dependent than in field-independent observers.

The idea that field dependence in upright perception might be due to a visual-vestibular interaction seemed consistent with other evidence as well. By the mid-1970s, it was clear from physiological, as well as perceptual data, that movements of the visual field are capable of driving the vestibular system (Dichgans & Brandt, 1974; Dichgans, Held, Young, & Brandt, 1972).

Much of the perceptual research on moving displays has been done with illusions of self-motion, for example the illusion of self-rotation called circularvection. A subjective experience of self-rotation is normally produced in the dark when the vestibular system is stimulated by rotating an observer around the long axis of the body when aligned with the vertical, as in a barber chair. But the same perceptual experience can also be produced as an illusion of self-rotation or circularvection by rotating a vertically striped drum in the opposite direction around a stationary observer. By the mid-1970s it seemed clear that the illusion of self-rotation that is experienced while watching a rotating drum is due to a visual driving of the vestibular system. Moreover, there was also evidence linking this work to the field dependence dimension. Field-dependent people are particularly susceptible to visually induced illusions of self-motion (Witkin & Goodenough, 1981).

Perceptual research on moving displays has also been done with illusions of object motion (Nilsson, Magnusson, & Vasko, 1972). The oculogyral illusion may be cited as an example of this type. The oculogyral illusion involves the apparent motion and displacement of a point of light objectively located straight ahead of, and rotating with, the observer in an otherwise dark room. The oculogyral illusion is a perceptual response to vestibular stimulation, like the subjective experience of self-rotation in the dark, and susceptibility to this illusion is sometimes used as a measure of vestibular sensitivity. Moreover, Nilsson et al. found that susceptibility to the oculogyral illusion is related to field dependence. In this case, field dependent people, who are most susceptible to the rod-and-frame illusion, are least susceptible to the oculogyral illusion.

These findings were difficult to understand in terms of a cognitive disembedding ability. Instead, they suggested to Hy that the rod-and-frame illusion is due to a visual driving of the vestibular system and that individual differences in upright perception may be determined by the relative importance assigned to visual and vestibular stimuli in resolving the perceptual conflict (Witkin & Goodenough, 1981). This visual-vestibular interpretation is a more specific form of Hy's original cue-conflict theory of field dependence in upright perception.

As evidence accumulated on the nature of individual differences in upright perception and on the greater interpersonal autonomy of field independent people, the construct of self-nonself differentiation became increasingly more important in Hy's thinking about the field dependence dimension. With increasing segregation of the self from the nonself during the course of development, people become more independent in their social behavior and more independent in their use of gravitational cues in upright perception. It is as though an internal gyroscope develops, allowing a person to function without being affected very much by the ever-changing visual world in upright perception or by the ever-changing social world in interpersonal behavior (Goodenough, 1978).

After weighing these developments, Hy redefined field independence as a dimension of autonomy, or self-nonself differentiation expressed in upright perception and in social functioning (Witkin & Goodenough, 1981). In the current idiom of information processing theory, the question became, What sources of information does a person use to resolve ambiguities? For more field-dependent people, the answer seemed to be that they characteristically rely more on information that is perceived to come from the world of objects and people around them. Embedded-Figures Test performance was also reinterpreted in terms of a separate, but related, disembedding or restructuring dimension, representing the expression of greater differentiation in the cognitive ability domain.

In summary, as the interaction between concepts and data continued in the search for a more unified view of individual differences, the field-dependence dimension itself changed position in the pyramid of constructs from an initially specific description of performance in perceptual tests to a much more general dimension of self-nonself differentiation.

Central in Hy's work was his constant search for a less value-laden conception of individual differences. In his original cue-conflict theory of field dependence in upright perception, Hy saw a value-neutral dimension. Contours in the visual fields of ordinary experience are usually aligned with the gravitational vertical, and either body cues or cues from the visual field can lead to accurate perception. To be sure, there are some unusual situations, like the Rod-and-Frame Test, where reliance on body cues leads to better performance, and there are other unusual situations where reliance on visual cues leads to better performance. But, in general, field-dependent people evidently differ from field-independent people in *how* they perceive the upright, rather than in *how accurately* they perceive the upright.

Working from this early base, Hy became a leader among psychologists who sought to identify stylistic differences among people in perceptual and cognitive functioning. With the shift from a disembedded theory of field dependence back to a form of his original cue-conflict theory, Hy returned to a more value-neutral cognitive style conception, with special skills associated with each end of the continuum. On the basis of his many contacts with subjects, it seemed to Hy that field-independent people were often less effective socially than field-dependent people and were sometimes even inept and offensive in their interpersonal relationships. Although the field-independent person might have an adaptive advantage in the greater development of cognitive disembedding or restructuring ability, it seemed possible that the field-dependent person might have the advantage in the greater development of certain interpersonal competencies.

Motivated in part by an attempt to broaden perspectives on the cognitive style issue, Hy turned increasingly to cross-cultural research in his later years (Witkin & Berry, 1975). Initially, he compared cultures in order to test certain hypotheses about socialization factors in the development of field independence. But as his involvement with the cross-cultural approach increased, he became more and more interested in the adaptive advantages of field-dependent and field-independent ways of functioning in different cultural settings.

Most cross-cultural studies of subsistence-level cultures support the conclusion that hunting and gathering people tend to be more field independent than farming people. For example, the Eskimo hunters of the Arctic Wastelands of North America, and the Aboriginal hunters of the desert Wastelands of Australia are among the most field-independent peoples of the world.

These results suggested to Hy that the cognitive style that characterizes a cultural group is broadly tuned to the adaptive requirements of the ecocultural setting. In this view, the cognitive disembedding skills associated with a field independent cognitive style are more adaptive for the hunter, who is often required to extract information from the surrounding environmental context, to locate game, and to return home from the hunt. In contrast, the more sedentary existence of the farmer may require less disembedding skill. But the larger and more complexly organized social groups in which the farmer lives place greater demands on social-interpersonal skill. In this cross-cultural perspective, Hy saw the possibility of achieving a greater symmetry or balance with his new theory of field dependence (Witkin & Goodenough, 1981).

From his starting point as a laboratory investigator of perception, Hy's search for an understanding of individual differences in field dependence led him into areas literally spanning the range from biology to anthropology. Obviously, many new research directions were stimulated during the process. The fact that Hy Witkin was listed among the 100 authors most cited in the *Social Sciences Citation* index, is one objective measure of his influence. Another objective measure is the rapidly growing literature on field dependence, now listing over three thousand references. But, as impressive as they are, these lists hardly measure Hy's contribution to the behavioral sciences. If we of lesser genius are any more likely than we once were to see individual differences as an important issue, even in our simplest laboratory experiments, then some credit must be added to the list. If we are any more likely to consider how our subjects' personalities may influence the results of even our simplest experiments, then some credit must be added. If we are any more likely to think of individual differences in value-neutral terms, then some credit must be added. If we are any more likely to think of relationships among biological, psychological, and social phenomena, then some credit must be added.

In sum, if our understanding of individual differences is any better today than it was in 1940, then some measure of credit must be added to the list of Hy Witkin's contributions.

REFERENCES

Asch, S. E., & Witkin, H. A. (1948a). Studies in space orientation I. Perception of the upright with displaced visual fields. *Journal of Experimental Psychology, 38,* 325–337.

Asch, S. E., & Witkin, H. A. (1948b). Studies in space orientation II. Perception of the upright with displaced visual fields and with body tilted. *Journal of Experimental Psychology, 38,* 455–477.

Bischof, N. (1974). Optic-vestibular orientation to the vertical. In H. H. Kornhuber (Ed.), *Handbook of sensory physiology: Vestibular system: Part 2.* New York: Springer-Verlag.

Dichgans, J., & Brandt, T. (1974). The psychophysics of visually induced perception of self-motion and tilt. In F. O. Schmitt & F. G. Worden (Eds.), *The neurosciences: Third study program.* Cambridge, MA: MIT Press.

Dichgans, J., Held, R., Young, L. R., & Brandt, T. (1972). Moving visual scenes influence the apparent direction of gravity. *Science, 178,* 1217–1219.

Goodenough, D. R. (1978). Field dependence. In H. London & J. Exner (Eds.), *Dimensions of personality.* New York: Wiley.

Goodenough, D. R., Sigman, E., Oltman, P. K., Rosso, J., & Mertz, H. (1979). Eye torsion in response to a tilted visual stimulus. *Vision Research, 19,* 1177–1179.

Hughes, P. C. (1973). The influence of the visual field upon the visual vertical in relation to ocular torsion of the eyes. *Dissertation Abstracts International, 33,* 4686B.

Nilsson, A., Magnusson, P., & Vasko, T. (1972). *Reflexive versus perceptual regulation: An investigation of nystagmus, oculogyral illusion, motion-and-median plane and rod-and-frame.* Sweden: Lund University Psychological Research Bulletin.

Witkin, H. A., & Asch, S. E. (1948a). Studies in space orientation III. Perception of the upright in the absence of a visual field. *Journal of Experimental Psychology, 38,* 603–614.

Witkin, H. A., & Asch, S. E. (1948b). Studies in space orientation IV. Further experiments on perception of the upright with displaced visual fields. *Journal of Experimental Psychology, 38,* 762–782.

Witkin, H. A., & Berry, J. W. (1975). Psychological differentiation in cross-cultural perspective. *Journal of Cross-Cultural Psychology, 6,* 4–87.

Witkin, H. A., Dyk, R. B., Faterson, H. F., Goodenough, D. R., & Karp, S. K. (1962). *Psychological Differentiation.* New York: Wiley.

Witkin, H. A., & Goodenough, D. R. (1977). Field dependence and interpersonal behavior. *Psychological Bulletin, 84,* 661–689.

Witkin, H. A., & Goodenough, D. R. (1981). *Cognitive styles: Essence and origins. Field dependence and field independence.* New York: International Universities Press.

Witkin, H. A., Goodenough, D. R., & Oltman, P. K. (1979). Psychological differentiation: Current status. *Journal of Personality and Social Psychology, 37,* 1127–1145.

Witkin, H. A., Lewis, H. B., Hertzman, M., Machover, K., Meissner, P. B., and Wapner, S. (1954). *Personality through perception: An experimental and clinical study.* New York: Harper & Brothers.

3 Some Implications of Witkin's Teaching for Sleep and Dreaming Psychophysiology

Mario Bertini
University of Rome

In this chapter, I wish to remember and to make personal testimony to a friend and a teacher — to illustrate the way in which Hy's thought, and my collaboration with him inspired a great part of my scientific work in a specific sector of psychophysiology, i.e., sleep and dreaming.

Witkin introduced me to this fascinating area. I had been collaborating with him for almost a year, involved in studying some structural factors of the Rod-and-Frame Test, when he proposed a digression into the field of dreaming. I still remember the details. Hy's words were more or less the following:

> As you know, we are investigating the dream dynamic in relation to field dependence. The methodological direction basically involves seeing how field-independent and field-dependent subjects transform an emotional film stimulus presented before sleep into dreams as they are reported upon awakenings from the REM stage. What we know is the input and the output; what is lacking is an understanding of the intermediate, digestive, process which, for example, could be carried out at that peculiar stage of transition from wake to sleep known as hypnagogic period. Mario, would you be interested in working on this with Helen Lewis and me?

These were the years, 1962, 1963, and 1964, when the startling discoveries of Aserinsky, Dement and Kleitman on the REM phase found a meaningful echo and stimulus at Downstate Medical Center. I was captured by this still pioneering climate. I didn't know what I was coming up against by involving myself with sleep.

We set out to formulate a technique that would facilitate the emergence and recording of hypnagogic thought. By means of a so-called reverie technique,[1] we discovered a series of intensely suggestive thought nuances in a state of peculiarly reduced vigilance. As in a culture terrain, it seemed possible to see outside the dream state some proliferation of a whole repertoire of symbolism from a psychoanalytic manual.

One evening, with that enthusiasm and vitality which maintained the powerful motivation of those near him, Witkin said, "Mario, you are involved in some of the most important issues of present-day psychology. I'm serious! ...Believe me!" And you didn't know if the scale was balanced more toward his sublime sense of humor or toward his convinced and obstinate optimism.

Seeing a continuous symbolic restitution of film messages with explicit sexual connotations was like finding experimental confirmation of Freud's clinical intuitions and gave us a methodology to deepen the dynamic aspects of symbolic transformations. However, I would like to focus on investigations more specifically linked to field dependence that I have carried out in the past years together with my colleagues, under the more or less direct influence of Hy's thought.

Three major theoretical-methodological references of great interest are at the root of this thought.

Witkin's first lesson has to do with *annoyance with nosology*. Witkin's thought reflects a basic research effort of coherent principles, of unifying structures that cut, so to speak, vertically through the usual horizontal nosographic categories. These principles broke up the static partitioning in which personality theorists had become rooted. Such theorizing followed an arc of reflections that swept from traditional European psychiatry to the philosophy of Anglo-Saxon elementarism and uncovered the dynamic key of functional organization. Instead of considering personality as a building resulting from and breakable into all of its separate floors, Witkin taught us to look at its deeper structure, which penetrates far and wide, organizing the floors from the inside into a design of a unique order.

---

[1]A description of the technique can be seen in Bertini (1968) or in Bertini, Lewis, & Witkin (1969). In synthesis, white noise is fed into the subjects' ears at the same time that they see a reddish homogeneous field. While the subjects are lying down in this special situation, they are asked to keep on talking continuously. Instructions of the following kind are given: "This is a study of imagination. You will be in the bed here. These cut ping-pong balls will be placed over your eyes. You will also wear these earphones through which you will hear a uniform, continuous sound. Please try to be as still as you can on the bed. It is also important that you keep your eyes open during the entire procedure. What I would like you to do, when we are ready, is to start talking and to keep on talking. Talk about anything you please. Talk about anything that you see, anything you hear. In other words, any images you have and anything you feel in your body. The important thing is that you keep on talking continuously. Are there any questions you have?" A thorough tape recording is made of the subject's speech.

Nourished by this functional approach, instead of looking at the imagined palace of the states of consciousness with the eye of the nosologist, who distinguishes and separates waking from sleeping and from dreaming, I preferred to look through its large floors, searching for unifying principles, for organizational coherence. The observation, facilitated by our technique, that dream-like productions could emerge during the day, impelled me to ask myself if the REM stage was linked strictly to sleep, or if it might not continue in some form even during the day (Bertini, 1964). More specifically, the doubt originated from the surprise of seeing how — though in a condition of reduced vigilance, but certainly not in the sleep cycle — it was possible for the subject to verbalize thoughts that, in many aspects, appeared to be like dreaming thoughts.[2]

Reflecting on the structural conditions of our technique, I was impressed by the similarities to the paradoxical situation typical of REM, where the organism reaches that dynamic equilibrium between withdrawal of energy from the external world (block of external information and drastic relaxation of musculature) and the involvement of energy at the internal level (intense cortical activation). In a somewhat comparable way, in our *reverie* technique, the subject is placed in a paradoxical situation of immobility or muscle relaxation — instructed to be as still as possible — while being intensely activated in internal mental orientation — stimulated to speak continuously. The outside world disappears in the absolute destructuralization of environmental stimuli.

Perhaps the same dynamic relationship between brain activation or arousal and motor inhibition could be profitably utilized for understanding a variety of the so-called altered states of consciousness. Basically similar is the dynamic situation classically considered as responsible for Silberer's (1951) autosymbolic phenomenon, the effort to think while in the transition from waking to sleeping that makes for a symbolic transformation from ideational thought to concrete imagery. The task of discovering functional unifying mechanisms of similar experiences through the different states appears very difficult. However, as the experience with the reverie technique continued, I became increasingly convinced that the rigid welding between dreaming and REM phase, as it appeared to take shape in those years, reflected more a schematic exigency than a reading of reality.

Since the beginning of the so-called REM era, the hypothesis had been repeatedly advanced that the functions associated with this stage, namely dreaming, were not strictly confined to it. Later on this suggestion was developed in various ways, both on a theoretical and on an empirical basis. In spite

---

[2]I still remember the enthusiasm with which Helen, Hy and I listened repeatedly to a passage where, after speaking in a more or less rational and ordinary way, one subject gave the impression of entering a dream state, i.e., he was "inside a green bottle in a pink cloud."

of its relevance for psychopathology and for a circadian theory of knowledge, we must admit that not enough steps have been taken along this path.

The second lesson, inspired by Witkin's thought, was that of *individual differences*. Where laboratory experimentalists tend to cancel out differences among individuals as undesirable "noise" in the purity of analyzing the process, Witkin focuses on these differences to understand better both the individual and the process itself.

The story of field dependence was born in the context of a discussion on whether visual or postural factors were more important in the perceptual determination of verticality. In that context, Witkin asked himself, "Important for whom?" This apparently simple question created a wealth of consequences for the theory and praxis of research. It seems that the same question may also apply to the sleeping and waking psychophysiology.

Instead of focusing attention on general laws, such as the correspondence between states and thinking modalities, we might inquire about the possibility of consistent individual differences in the degree of such correspondence. Instead of asking whether dream-like mentation belongs to REM, thought-like mentation to non-REM, and rational thinking to waking states, we might appropriately ask whether there are some individuals for whom dream mentation is strictly associated with REM and whether for some others this association is much less strict and rigid. Following this lead, we proceeded with the hypothesis that a greater or lesser level of fusion or of separation between sleep-wake subsystems is somehow linked to — and possibly is another expression at the psychophysiological level — of the field dependence dimension. This hypothesis led to a series of other investigations.

First to come to light in the initial reverie experiments that were conducted with Hy Witkin and Helen Lewis was the different degree to which certain subjects, at an extreme, slipped easily into dream-like production in comparison with others who maintained quite lucid, rational thought. The first observations indicated that subjects showing a greater tendency for sleep operations during wakefulness were more field dependent, and subjects showing a lesser tendency in this direction were more field independent. These findings led to a further study. In an investigation conducted in Rome, Bertini, de Martin Gregolini, and Bellagamba (1971), using subjects at the extremes of the field dependence/independence dimension, observed that, in reverie sessions, field-dependent subjects were judged higher in all subscales of dreamlike mentation than field-independent subjects (See Fig. 3.1).

With a different approach, using Bett's Mental Imagery Test, we had findings supporting the idea that less differentiated, field dependent subjects in wakefulness tend toward forms of thought more consonant with those of dreaming sleep. (See Table 3.1.)

Starker (1973) demonstrated that less differentiated (field-dependent) subjects have more bizarre experiences in their daydreams.

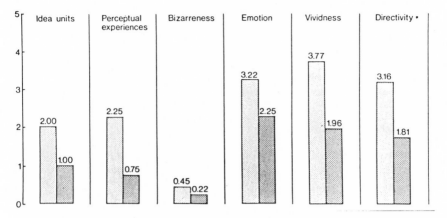

FIG. 3.1   Content analysis of free associations under the influence of one technique (high scores = more dreamlike); Darker columns = field-independent subjects (*n* = 14); Lighter columns = field-dependent subjects (*n* = 12) *p*<001; High score = low directivity.

TABLE 3.1
Bett's Mental Imagery Questionnaire (shortened form)

	Session I	Session II	Session III
FI Ss (n = 20)	86.25	89.06	95.37
FD Ss (n = 20)	84.46	86.69	82.92

(Low scores = more vivid imagery)
FI and FD subjects differ significantly at *p* < .01 on each of the three test sessions

The hypothesis of greater presence of sleep during wakefulness in less differentiated (field-dependent) subjects, and of a greater separation between states in more differentiated (field-independent subjects) was expanded in the opposite direction; the greater presence of wakefulness during sleep. We have shown (Boccalon et al., 1976) a significantly greater intrusion of periods of wakefulness during sleep for less differentiated than for more differentiated subjects. Extending such a hypothesis, we further evaluated the intrusion of non-REM (NREM) sleep and waking (W) within REM sleeping (Torre et al., 1976).

As shown in Fig. 3.2, less differentiated subjects display higher levels of intrusion of NREM sleep and wakefulness in the REM phase on each of the experimental nights (both on baseline nights and after recovery from REM dep-

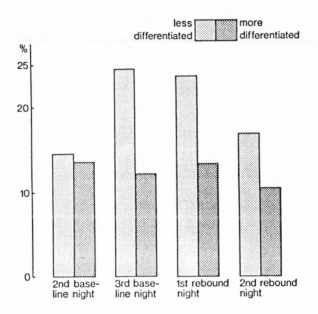

FIG. 3.2   Mean percentage of NREM + W intrusion values within REM periods.

rivation). These data indicate a greater fusion between wake and sleep subsystems in less differentiated, field-dependent subjects.

In the same study, the hypothesis was further extended on a dynamic level of observation by experimentally forcing relationships between systems using the REM deprivation method. As indicated in Fig. 3.3, on the second recovery night, more differentiated subjects show a significant effect of REM rebound ($p < .05$), whereas no recovery effect was observed in less differentiated subjects. I believe that these data, like those of other workers (Cartwright, Monroe, & Palmer, 1967; Gillin, Buchsbaum, & Jacobs, 1974), show the tendency of more differentiated subjects to postpone REM operations to the specific REM stages of the following night without diffusing them in other sleep or wake stages. In contrast, this diffusion probably happens more easily for less differentiated subjects. This interpretation is supported by the course of imagery in the days following REM deprivation. Indeed, a statistically significant difference in response to REM deprivation can be observed between the two groups in imagery vividness as measured in a morning testing.

After REM deprivation, less differentiated subjects show an increase in imagery vividness in the morning, whereas no similar spilling over can be observed in more differentiated subjects. In the morning following recovery nights, more differentiated subjects show a slight decrease in their imagery vividness parallel to their increase in REM stage. (See Torre et al., 1976).

From these empirical findings, the hypothesis of substantial individual differences in degree of separation between waking and sleep operations seems to receive support. Thus, to the generic model of so-called REM pressure on daytime, we might add a more specific structural one centered on individually diversified predispositions to transfer into the waking state the psychobiological operations typical of the sleep states, and vice versa.

This structural model also presents a significant connection with definite morbid conditions. As noted by Witkin (1965), in the case of psychotic breakdown, field-dependent subjects were more oriented towards hallucinatory symptoms than were the field-independent subjects, who appeared to be more prone to delusional symptoms.

Because these data were important for our model, we attempted to replicate this type of investigation, selecting with particular care from psychiatric patients, two groups of subjects showing opposite symptoms; one group with highly hallucinatory manifestations and the other with a structure of organized delusions. All were subjected to tests for field dependence. The results presented in Table 3.2 provide a dramatic confirmation of our hypothesis (Bertini, Ruggeri, & Scepi, 1982).

Consistent with what was observed through the reverie technique in normal subjects, psychotic field-dependent subjects, while awake, tend to manifest the pictorial hallucinatory, dream-like quality typical of sleep functioning. Field-independent patients, on the other hand, consistent with what was observed in their reverie mentation, show less disposition to that quality.

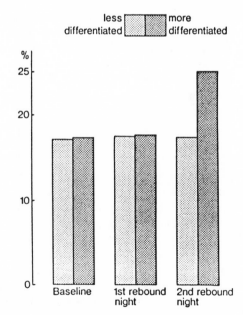

FIG. 3.3 Differences in REM percentages between less and more differentiated subjects.

TABLE 3.2
Range and Mean Performance Scores on Field Dependency Tests of
Psychotics With Different Symptoms

	Hallucinations Prevalent (N = 15)	Delusions Prevalent (N = 15)
Group Embedded	0.73	6.80
Figures Test	(0–4)	(1–17)
Human Figure	1.12	3.66
Drawing	(1–3)	(2–5)
Block Design	9.19	20.40
	(3–19)	(6–30)

Comparisons between patient groups significant on each test at $p < .01$ by the Rank Sums Test

Although in a delusional mode of organization, they tend to preserve the thought-like form of mentation typical of the waking state.

Individual differences in the continuum of field dependence were ordered by Witkin in terms of the Wernerian (Werner, 1940, 1957) framework of differentiation, and evaluation of the *developmental dimension* constitutes Witkin's third great lesson (Witkin, Dyk, Faterson, Goodenough, & Karp (1962); Witkin & Goodenough (1981). The importance of applying a developmental approach also to sleep-wake processes cannot be overemphasized. The formal construct of differentiation applied to this specific area should consider that sleep, dreaming stage, and wakefulness are fused at birth in a primitive, common matrix where sleep and dreaming prevail, in which, little by little, increasingly prolonged periods of wakefulness occur until an articulated separation of subsystem is reached. As McGinty (1979) put it, "Ontogeny is characterized by the gradual emergence of distinct states from an undifferentiated pattern of physiological organization, and the graduate recruitment of state-related characteristics" (p. 171). The individual differences observed in the degree of separation (or specialization) between sleeping and waking operations might be understood as an expression of different levels of development attained. Our findings are consistent with this hypothesis.

To illustrate conclusively and to develop further the proposed framework of greater or lesser differentiation between subsystems, one should consider the relationship of the circadian rest-activity cycle to the ultradian dream-sleep cycle as described by Hobson (1982) (although in a quite different connection). Figure 3.4 illustrates two different modalities of these relationships: the first, in the upper portion, which I propose to consider as characteristic for more differentiated subjects; the second, in the lower portion, which I propose as typical of less differentiated subjects. In the first modality, that associated with more differentiated subjects, due to the large amplitude of the circadian oscillator, the dream-sleep oscillator can easily emerge during sleeping; although still present, it cannot ever reach the threshold during waking. A clearcut distinction results between what belongs to sleeping and what belongs to waking.

In the second modality, typical of less differentiated subjects, due to the low amplitude of the circadian oscillator, the dream oscillator can only partially express itself during sleep. However, it can easily overcome the threshold during waking. In this latter case, therefore, more fusion and less separation result between what belongs to sleeping states and what belongs to waking states.

The attainment of an optimal amplitude of the circadian rest-activity oscillator constitutes, in our perspective, a specific developmental task. The individual differences described previously should be considered as extremes of a continuum from poor to high levels of system differentiation.

In summary, a radical revision is applicable to the old schema of waking and sleeping states, with their stereotyped correlation with thought processes. A basic contribution of modern sleep research is the systematic demonstration that much of waking activity is present in sleeping, and much of sleeping activity is present in waking. In the near future it may not even make

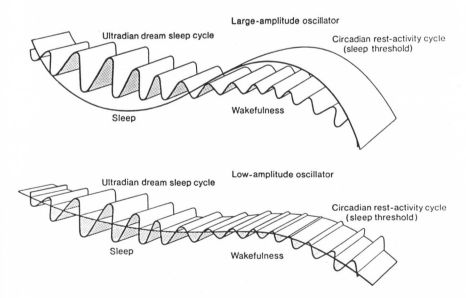

FIG. 3.4   Distinct modalities of relationships between the circadian rest-activity cycle, and the ultradian dream-sleep cycle, according to differentiation degree, i.e., field dependency. Patterns for more differentiated (field-independent) and less-differentiated (field-dependent) subjects are depicted in the upper and lower portion, respectively.

much sense to speak (*sic et simpliciter*) of sleeping, waking, and dreaming states.

A certain coherence in state patterning is to be expected in the adjusted organism. However, this coherence is a product of gradual development from a situation of relative fusion between states. Typically, this situation of fusion maintains itself in the narcoleptic syndrome (Passouant, Halberg, Genicot, Popoviciu, & Baldy-Moulinier, 1969) and in other sleeping-waking abnormalities.

In line with Witkin's thinking, my specific proposal is to extend attention beyond sleep disorders and to look for the varieties of ways (differences in degree as well as in modality) through which development can orient and determine waking and sleeping state organization and cycling in different individuals. Following this path, I am more and more convinced that dream-like thinking (as one of the two typical modalities in information processing) runs through all of the states, although in different proportion within states and between individuals.

Whether the presence of dream-like thinking is desirable or not greatly depends on specific mechanisms of integration with the other modality – that is, the more rational one – of the thinking process. Following a developmental approach, we should take into account not only the differentiation aspects between systems but also the integrative ones. Inasmuch as dreaming is present either in attenuated or overt form during waking, and rational thinking is present during sleeping, what can be said about the integration between these different modalities of thinking processes at the different levels of development and in the different stages of the circadian cycle? Although poorly investigated, these are major problems for a circadian theory of knowledge with many relevant implications both for normal and for morbid operations.

REFERENCES

Bertini, M. (1964). La moderna psicofisiologia del sogno. *Archivio di Psicologia Neurologia e Psichiatria, XXV, VI,* 535–599.

Bertini, M. (1968). Processi di trasformazione simbolica nel periodo del dormiveglia e del sogno. *IKON, 65–66,* 9–33.

Bertini, M., Lewis, H., & Witkin, H. (1969). Some preliminary observations with an experimental procedure for the study of hypnagogic and related phenomena. In C. Tart (Ed.), *Altered states of consciousness.* N.Y.: Wiley.

Bertini, M., deMartin Gregolini, H., & Bellagamba, A. (1971). Studi psicofisiologici e di personalita sui processi di elaborazione simbolica di materiale filmico in condizioni ipnagogico-simili. In M. Bertini (Ed.), *Psicofisiologia del sonno e del sogno.* Milano: Vita e Pensiero.

Bertini, M., Ruggeri, G., & Scepi, A. (1982). Sintomatologia allucinatoria e delirante nella prospettiva della differenziazione psicologica. *Psicologia Clinica, 1,* 77–97.

Boccalon, R., Bergonzi, P., DeRosa, G., Natalini, P., Torre, A., Vallania, M., & Bertini, M. (1976). Sleep, obesity and psychological differentiation. In W. Koella & P. Levin (Eds.), *Sleep*. Basel: Karger.

Cartwright, R., Monroe, L., & Palmer, C. (1967). Individual differences in response to REM deprivation. *Archives of General Psychiatry, 16,* 297-303.

Gillin, J., Buchsbaum, M., & Jacobs, L. (1974). Partial deprivation schizophrenia and field articulation. *Archives of General Psychiatry, 30,* 653-663.

Hobson, A. (1982). Implicazioni cliniche dell'ipotesa dell'interazione reciproca nel controllo del ciclo del sonno. In M. Bertini & C. Violani (Eds.), *Cervello e soqno*. Milano: Feltrinelli.

McGinty, L. (1979). Ontogenetic and clinical studies of sleep state organization and dissociation. In R. Drucker-Colin, M. Shkurovich, & M. B. Sterman (Eds.), *The functions of sleep*. N.Y.: Academic Press.

Passouant, P., Halberg, F., Genicot, R., Popoviciu, L., & Baldy-Moulinier, M. (1969). La périodicité des accès narcoleptiques et le rythme ultradien du sommeil rapide. *Review of Neurology, 121,* 155-164.

Silberer, H. (1951). Report on a method of eliciting and observing certain symbolic hallucination phenomena. In D. Rapaport (Ed.), *Organization and pathology of thought*. New York: Columbia University Press.

Starker, S. (1973). Aspects of inner experience: Autokinesis, daydreaming, dream recall, and cognitive style. *Perceptual Motor Skills, 36,* 663-673.

Torre, A., Caringi, G., Dazzi, N., Roccioletti, G., Rivolta, L., Zulli, A., & Bertini, M. (1976). Psychological differentiation and sleep-wake differentiation. In W. Koella & P. Levin (Eds.), *Sleep*. Basel: Karger.

Werner, H. (1940). *Comparative psychology of mental development*. NY: Harper. (2nd Ed., 1948, Chicago: Follett; 3rd Ed., 1957, NY: International Universities Press.)

Werner, H. (1957). The concept of development from a comparative and organismic point of view. In D. B. Harris (Ed.), *The concept of development*. Minneapolis: University of Minnesota Press.

Witkin, H. (1965). Psychological differentiation and forms of pathology. *Journal of Abnormal Psychology, 70,* 317-336.

Witkin, H., Dyk, R., Faterson, H., Goodenough, D., & Karp, P. (1962). *Psychological differentiation*. New York: Wiley.

Witkin, H. A., & Goodenough, D. R. (1981). *Cognitive styles: Essence and origins. Field dependence and field independence*. New York: International Universities Press.

4 Individual Differences: Cerebral Structure and Cognitive Characteristics

Luigi Pizzamiglio
Pierluigi Zoccolotti
University of Rome

Within the realm of psychology, there has been extensive investigation of individual differences; these studies have had different orientations in various historical periods. The emphasis has been on both cognitive and emotional differences and on observable differences in the organization of personality structure. Similarly, since the last century, the literature on the central nervous system (CNS) has evidenced findings of great individual variability, observable at both the macroscopic and microscopic level. However, interest in a systematic examination of interindividual anatomic differences has only recently received an important stimulus. This is, in part, due to the development of technical means that allow for live exploration of several structural variations.

The conceptually more interesting question is whether structural differences that can be seen in the CNS of different individuals have functional significance; that is, can these variations in the CNS explain, at least in part, some behavioral differences observable in normal subjects and in subjects with cerebral lesions?

The possible relationship between the organization modality of the CNS and individual behavioral characteristics can be approached also from the opposite perspective. One can ask whether there are differences in the psychological functioning of the individual that are correlated or capable of predicting different organization modalities of the CNS.

INDIVIDUAL DIFFERENCES IN CEREBRAL STRUCTURE

The literature on the anatomy of man's cerebral structures is rich with information on both interindividual and intraindividual differences for many parameters regarding analogous structures in the two cerebral hemispheres. Reviews by Whitaker and Selnes (1976), Le May and Geschwind (1978), and Rubens (1977) report data analytically accumulated through strictly anatomic studies and through studies using the most recent neuro-radiological techniques.

The weight of the brain of a mentally and physically normal individual may vary from 680 to 1938 grams (Wilder, 1889). The majority of the studies cited by LeMay and Geschwind (1978) show systematic asymmetry in the weight of the cerebral hemispheres, the right hemisphere having the advantage.

Although somewhat irrelevant variations in the total surface of the cortex have been described, more consistent differences exist in the length of the two hemispheres in adult human subjects. In fact, the left cortex is longer than the right in 7 out of 10 cases, shorter in 2 out of 10, and equal in 1 out of 10 cases (Connolly, 1950).

Studies of autoptic material (Inglessis, 1919) and of data obtained with computerized axial tomography (Hounsfield, Ambrose, Perry & Bridges, 1973) showed a tendency toward greater protrusion of the right frontal pole than of the left, accompanied by greater width of the same pole; greater width and protrusion of the left than of the right occipital pole has been described with greater regularity. Differences in occipital structures (length and width) are more marked in right-handed than in left-handed subjects and are also present in infant brains.

In normal adult subjects, the lateral ventricles are usually wider on the left side, and, in particular, the occipital horns in the majority of right-handed subjects are longer on the left. However, the inverse pattern is observed in left-handed and ambidexterous subjects (McRae, Braunch & Milner, 1968).

Remarkable individual variations have been described with regard to cerebral gyri and sulci. Thus, Roland's fissure (where the upper and lower parts develop independently during the fetal period) may appear interrupted (Cunningham, 1892), and the anterior-posterior dislocations may be observed relative to its placement (Mickle, 1898). Similarly, Cunningham emphasizes how the number of gyri originating from Silvio's fissure may vary greatly from subject to subject. The same author describes Silvio's left fissure as usually longer than its contro-lateral. Also, the posterior part of the fissure folds upward at a more acute angle, and its end protrudes higher into the right than into the left hemisphere (LeMay & Culebras, 1972; Rubens, Mahowald, & Hutton, 1976). This tendency is observed in approximately

80% of right-handed subjects, while in 25% of cases the two ends reach the same height. On the contrary, approximately 70% of left-handed subjects show a symmetrical pattern on the two sides. This configuration of Silvio's fissure has greater fullness on the left side of the parietal structures and particularly in the posterior portion of the postcentral gyrus. In this case, the configuration described is inverted in left-handed subjects (LeMay & Geschwind, 1978).

Neuropsychologists have been most attracted to research concerned with differences between the two hemispheres in the temporal planum dimension because of their potential functional relevance. Pfeifer (1936) noted that the left temporal planum was larger than the right. Geschwind and Levitsky (1968), studying 100 adult brains, documented that in 65 cases the left temporal planum was fuller than the right, in 11 it was smaller, and in 24 there was no difference. These data were subsequently confirmed in studies by Teszner, Tzavaras, Gruner and Hecaen (1972), Wada (1969), Wada, Clarke and Hamm (1975), and Witelson and Pallie (1973), with the following important specifications: (a) greater fullness of the left temporal planum is present both in the adult and infant brain; and (b) differences between the two temporal planum are more frequent in males than in females.

Whitaker and Selnes (1976) and Le May and Geschwind (1978) also report extensive findings regarding important individual variations in both the location of arterial structures and venous drainage between the two hemispheres. The noteworthy variations in the arterial system seem to be particularly important in that they may contribute to explaining some apparent difficulties in correlations between cerebral lesions and observable clinical symptomatology.

Le May and Geschwind (1978) discuss critically the functional significance that can be attributed to these individual and interhemispheric differences taken as a whole. First, they clarify the point that macroscopic differences may have low significance if unaccompanied by microscopic documentation demonstrating how this diversity corresponds to a different cellular structure and thus, probably, to a different pattern of functional connections. In fact, diversity that can be shown only at the macroscopic level may simply be the result of a different folding up of the cortex, with the cellular structure remaining identical. With this interpretative caution, the authors maintain that, at least with regard to structural differences in the temporal planum, Wernicke's area, associated with language, is, in fact, more developed in the left hemisphere.

On the basis of their findings, Le May and Geschwind (1978) made the following speculative inferences:

1. Interhemispheric differences observable in various individuals can be seen from the first days of life and thus, probably should be interpreted as ge-

netically determined and not as a consequence of interaction between the CNS and the external environment.

2. The asymmetrical hemispheres can be described as a continuum, and, thus, can be shown in two opposite directions and with different intensity. These anatomic differences may constitute the support of several degrees of functional specialization and are not in agreement with the hypothesis of an absolute functional specialization of one hemisphere over the other.

3. Anatomic differences between the two hemispheres, studied by means of several parameters previously described, tend to be less frequent and less accentuated in absolute values in left-handers than in right-handers. Thus, the authors conclude that in left-handed subjects cerebral organization may be different than in right-handed subjects.

This hypothesis is compatible with several observations on differential clinical incidence of aphasia in left-hemisphere lesions in right- and left-handers (99% and 60%, respectively) and on the differential functional recovery of right- and left-handed aphasic patients (Hecaen & Ajuiriaguerra, 1964; Zangwill, 1960). Approximately 25% of the aphasic patients described by Luria (1972) show good functional recovery: this better recovery is predictable considering the presence of left-handedness in the patients or in their parentage, rather than considering the extensiveness of the lesion. The percentage of subjects with greater functional equipotential, inferred from more rapid recovery of linguistic capabilities, is compatible with the percentage of anatomic equivalences described between the temporal planum of the two hemispheres.

Taken together, these observations present interesting study possibilities, in particular with regard to anatomic characteristics and different functional performances in various subjects. However, the only behavioral variable studied directly in relation to cortical asymmetry is represented by hand dominance. This is due, in part, to the relative ease with which this dimension can be measured and, in part, to the tremendous amount of knowledge acquired in the clinical and experimental realm on the higher predictive capacity of this variable. Certainly, this approach could become stimulating if it were possible to study individual structural differences in relation to other functional and behavioral parameters.

COGNITIVE DIFFERENCES IN CNS ORGANIZATION

As stated previously, there is another approach to the study of how individual differences, measured by behavioral parameters, relate to different modalities of functional, and possibly anatomic, organization of the CNS. Above all, theoretical constructs and appropriate behavioral measures capable of describing the modality of functioning that reliably characterizes individual psychological functioning, must be singled out. In the psychological domain, the study of cognitive styles seems particularly appropriate for this type of investigation.

Cognitive Style

By *cognitive style* we mean the consistent modes of functioning shown by individuals in their perceptual and intellective activity. The concept of cognitive style accentuates the "how" rather than the "how much" of behavior; thus, it describes modes of information processing rather than different levels of performance.

The most famous and most widely used cognitive style is that of field dependence-independence (Witkin, Dyk, Faterson, Goodenough, & Karp, 1962). The original studies on this type of cognitive style were concerned with aspects of perceptual functioning of the individual. Here, we make reference to two of these perceptual situations because chronologically they were studied first, because an enormous amount of data has been gathered using them, and because the experiments to be described later are based on these types of measurements.

The first situation is the Rod-and-Frame Test (RFT). The subject, seated in a totally dark room, must bring to the vertical a luminous, initially slanted, rod surrounded by a luminous frame, which is also slanted. Individual performance on this test is described by a continuum that oscillates between two extremes. Some subjects, even in the presence of deviant perceptual information (slanted frame), are able to bring the luminous rod to a vertical, or almost vertical, position, whereas other subjects, strongly influenced by the position of the frame, orient the rod to the frame's slanted direction.

A second perpetual test consists of identifying simple figures in an embedding context (Embedded Figures Test, EFT). In this situation, the subject must single out a simple figure, seen previously in a larger and more complex figure that, due to its own internal structure, tends to hide the simple figure. Also, in this situation subjects tend to be located at either extreme of a continuum: some individuals easily recognize the simple figure in the complex one; others either fail to do so or require a great deal of time to make a correct identification.

These two situations share the common characteristic of requiring the subject to perceptually organize a part of the stimulus situation in the presence of a more complex or embedding background. Thus, individuals who have greater difficulty in extracting a simple figure from a background, also make more errors in judging verticality in the presence of a deviant visual field. In other terms, these subjects are strongly dominated by the general structure of the field of stimulation and have difficulty in perceiving a part separated from the complex organization of the stimulus. These individuals are defined as relatively more field dependent. At the other extreme are subjects who are able to recognize discrete elements as emerging from a structural perceptual field and to impose an autonomous perceptual organization relatively independent of the forces present in the external situation; such individuals are defined as field independent.

An approach that is relatively more field independent or relatively more field dependent is not specifically linked to only one sensory modality (visual), but is manifested also in different modalities, for example in tactile and auditory situations (Axelrod & Cohen, 1961; White, 1954; Witkin, Birnbaum, Lomonaco, Lehr, and Herman, 1968; Pizzamiglio and Carli, 1973). However, the field dependence-independence dimension does not extend to all perceptual and cognitive situations, but is manifested specifically when the task requires breaking an existing organization and regrouping several parts separately. In this regard, numerous factorial and correlative studies exist to show, for example, how performance on tests of field dependence-independence is not correlated with the ability to single out an item in a distracting context or to make simple discriminations between parts of the field (Karp, 1963; Witkin et al., 1962). It has also been shown how this perceptual style is independent of other cognitive capacities, such as verbal comprehension or other factors in the verbal sphere (Goodenough & Karp, 1961; Witkin, Moore, Goodenough, & Cox, 1977).

The field dependence-independence dimension is not limited to the perceptual situations heretofore illustrated. Various investigations have shown how a more independent approach on the RFT or EFT is correlated, in the cognitive domain, with greater ability to solve problems (for example, Duncker's (1945) problems) that require the reorganization of a situational context (Goodenough & Karp, 1961; Karp, 1963; Witkin et al., 1962).

An important point regarding the use of these measures as indicators of underlying cognitive style has to do with their high degree of stability over time. On the RFT, test-retest correlations have been obtained that approximate .90 even in retests carried out years later in youth and adulthood. Moreover, RFT performance appears relatively insusceptible to learning (Witkin, Goodenough, & Karp, 1967). In fact, variations can be observed only as a consequence of changes, such as the administration of drugs, sensorial isolation, and the administration of electric shock (Witkin, Oltman, Raskin, & Karp, 1971). Instead, performance on the EFT presents a change in absolute scores as a function of learning of the situation, but the scores of subjects in the retest condition maintain a very high level of correlation (Witkin et al., 1962).

One important question concerns the ontogenetic development of this psychological dimension: Is field dependence influenced by biological factors? Numerous studies have been carried out on the mechanisms that regulate the ontogenetic development of this cognitive style. Only research relevant to biological mechanisms of this psychological dimension will be summarized.

Studies by Stafford (1961), Hartlage (1970), Bock and Kolakowski (1973) and Corah (1965) hypothesized that visuo-spatial ability, such as spatial rotation or spatial visualization, (both of which are correlated with measures of field dependence), are regulated by a recessive gene on the X chromosome. These studies are based on the analysis of family correlations: In particular, mother-son and father-daughter correlations are significant for these spatial abilities, whereas the father-son correlation (where, the son's only X chromosome is provided by the mother) tends toward zero.

Even though this pattern of correlations is compatible with the hypothesis of a genetic control linked to the X chromosome, the methodology used does not allow for the complete elimination of other types of interpretation that, for example, explain the data as a function of different emotional relationships that can be established between parents and offspring of both sexes.

Using a different experimental paradigm, Goodenough, Gandini, Olkin, Pizzamiglio, Thayer & Witkin (1977) investigated the possible link between the X chromosome and field dependence-independence. Families with at least three sons and with the X chromosome marked for the XGa factor were examined. The hypothesis of a link between field dependence-independence and the X chromosome can be formulated experimentally in the following way: Two brothers with the same X chromosome (XGa + or XGa −) should show a greater resemblance (correlation) in the psychological characteristic under investigation than should two brothers with a different X chromosome. Using this methodology, Goodenough et al. (1977) observed that, with regard to the RFT and EFT, the correlation between brothers with the same X chromosome is significantly higher than that between brothers with a different X chromosome. Interestingly, this pattern was not observed for other measures of spatial ability (spatial rotation and visualization) nor for verbal comprehension. Further support for the hypothesis of a link between this psychological characteristic and the X chromosome can be found in a study on individuals with Turner's syndrome (Serra, Pizzamiglio, Boari & Spera, 1978). Women with 45XO cariotype were shown to be significantly more field dependent with respect to two control groups, one consisting of sterile and one of normal subjects with 46XX cariotype.

The field dependence-independence dimension of cognitive style was conceived by Witkin et al. (1962) as an expression of a more general construct of psychological differentiation. In short, differentiation represents a formal, salient organization of every psychological system. A characteristic aspect of a more differentiated system is that it demonstrates a greater level of segregation and specialization of the functions of the organism. A great number of studies have demonstrated, on the basis of the concept of differentiation, how a more or less field dependent cognitive style is correlated in predictable ways with individual differences in areas such as the organization of controls and defenses and the articulation of body schema. In this way, subjects who, on the RFT and the EFT, tend to perceive in a more articulated way also show a more articulated body schema (as expressed in designs of the human figure), and a greater definition of body limits (Witkin et al., 1962). The same subjects also show greater autonomy in interpersonal relationships, having internalized a series of schemas that guide them in their relations with others (Witkin & Goodenough, 1976), and more specialized control and defense mechanisms, for example, rationalization toward mass repression (Witkin et al., 1962).

Cognitive Style and Hemispheric Lateralization

The conceptualization of field dependence-independence as a manifestation of more general psychological differentiation can be utilized to formulate operative hypotheses about relationships between different individuals in the psychological and neurophysiological area. Palmer (1964), in a review of the extensive literature, holds that the specialization that can be observed in ontogenetic development of various parts of the brain determines greater functional localization. One can advance the hypothesis that, if there is a correlation between psychological and neurological differentiation of the individual, it can be expected that subjects with different degrees of psychological differentiation differ in a predictable way in degree of hemispheric lateralization, on the basis of the field dependence-independence model.

In particular, the general hypothesis of a relationship between differentiation at the psychological and neurophysiological level does not imply any directionality in hemispheric specialization. Instead, greater psychological differentiation associated with greater functional specialization in both hemispheres is expected, each according to its prevalent mode of information processing. Therefore, a thorough test of the hypothesis requires that measures of psychological differentiation be able to predict the degree of hemispheric specialization both in verbal and visuospatial situations. On the basis of this work, numerous studies employing different measures of hemispheric specialization have been carried out to study the problem.

Silverman, Adevai and McGough (1966) showed that a group of non-right-handed subjects were more field dependent than a group of clearly right-handed subjects. However, clearly left-handed and ambidexterous individuals were included in the group of non right handers. Pizzamiglio (1974) studied the same problem, comparing a group of clearly lateralized subjects (right handers) with a group of less clearly lateralized subjects (ambidexterous); the ambidexterous individuals were more field dependent than the right-handed individuals.

In the same research, Pizzamiglio (1974), using the dichotic stimulation technique with verbal material (three pairs of numbers) with the same subjects, found yet another demonstration of the relationship between degree of lateralization and field dependence. The superiority of the left hemisphere in mediating linguistic processes and the prevalent crossing of the acoustic pathways normally leads to a greater response to stimuli that arrive at the right ear when two different stimuli reach the two ears simultaneously (Kimura, 1967). The subjects who showed strong right-ear superiority (a relationship of 3 between left/right errors) were significantly more field independent on the RFT and EFT with respect to subjects' showing a smaller difference between the two ears (relationship between .80 and 1.20). Analogous results were reported by Waber (1976), who used a dichotic test with explosive CV syllables and a cognitive index that included the EFT and found greater lateralization in individuals who were more cognitively independent. However, this was not found by Oltman, Ehrlichman and Cox (1977), who utilized a dichotic test with five pairs of numbers, which provoked the discrepant result of a negative correlation between the performance of the two ears (Oltman, personal communication). Finally, Zoccolotti (1977) reported a significant correlation between the index of lateralization, Kuhn's (1973) phi in a dichotic test of three pairs of letters, and measures of field dependence for a sample of women but not for a sample of men.

Overall, these studies seem to agree with the hypothesis of a significant relationship between field dependence-independence and degree of hemispheric lateralization with regard to the analysis of verbal material and, thus, level of functional specialization of the left hemisphere. Other studies document the existence of an analogous relationship between field dependence and functional lateralization of the right hemisphere.

An observer comparing a whole face with two faces, one comprising the two left halves of the original faces and the other comprising the two right halves, normally tends to evaluate the "double right face" as resembling the original more than it does the "double left face." Gilbert and Bakan (1973) explain this fact by hypothesizing that, when a subject looks at a whole face in a real situation, the right half falls in the left visual hemifield, which projects the information to the right hemisphere, and which, as noted, is more effective in processing this type of stimulus (Rizzolatti, Umilta, & Berlucchi, 1971). Oltman et al. (1977) showed that the dominance of the right double face described by Gilbert and Bakan (1973) was present in more field-independent subjects than in dependent ones.

In a different sensory modality, Benton, Varney and Hamsher (1978) showed that the left hand is more accurate than the right in perceiving tactile stimuli with different orientations. They interpreted this superiority as a manifestation of the mediation of the right hemisphere for this task. In an attempt to verify the hypothesis of a relationship between cognitive differentiation and hemispheric specialization in the tactile sensory modality, Zoccolotti, Passafiume and Pizzamiglio (1979) employed Benton et al's (1978) technique on a group of normal right-handed subjects with no left-handed family members of either sex. The experimental task consisted of asking the subject to touch, alternately with the fingers of the right and left hand, two different sloping segments. Subsequently, the subject was asked to recognize, by means of multiple choice, the segments that had the same slant as those examined previously. The subjects were also administered the RFT, the EFT, the PFA verbal comprehension test (Thurstone & Thurstone, 1947), and a test of closure speed, i.e., the Gestalt Completion Test, which is similar to Street's test (Ekstrom, French, Harman & Dermen, 1976). Data were analyzed to compare subjects with scores higher or lower than the mean in each of the four tests administered. With regard to the RFT, the EFT, and the test of verbal comprehension, subjects above the mean showed a very clear left-hand superiority, similar to that evidenced by Benton, Varney and Hamsher (1978), whereas subjects with scores lower than the mean showed only a modest and nonsignificant left-hand superiority. However, no difference between the two hands was predictable when the subjects were divided on the basis of performance on the Gestalt Completion Test.

The results confirm the previously formulated hypothesis and cannot be explained in terms of general cognitive efficiency of the subject. An unexpected result is the predictive power of the verbal comprehension test, which may also suggest that measures of verbal differentiation are in some way indicators of hemispheric specialization. On the other hand, the experimental data show an unusually high correlation between measure of field dependence (EFT) and verbal comprehension, in contrast with that repeatedly observed in the literature (Witkin et al, 1962). However, the results may be explained as an effect of the covariance between the two tests, linked to the particular sample of subjects examined.

As already indicated, the general hypothesis predicts that a greater degree of psychological differentiation is associated with greater specialization in both hemispheres, each according to the predominant mode of information processing. Whereas the data reported up to now are compatible with the model presented, a verification, including a measure of degree of hemispheric specialization, takes on particular relevance for both verbal and visuospatial stimuli in the same group of subjects.

Zoccolotti and Oltman (1978) presented a group of right-handed male subjects with the experimental situation described by Rizzolatti, et al. (1971). In two experimental sessions the subject was presented first letters and then faces tachistoscopically to both hemifields. In both cases the subject was trained to respond by pressing a button as rapidly as possible for only two letters or faces out of four possible alternatives. The experimental group was divided in two, i.e., field dependents and field independents, based on RFT and EFT performance. In the case of the field-independent subjects, the results are similar to those described by Rizzolatti et al. (1971): Reaction times for recognition of letters are significantly more rapid for right hemifield presentation (left hemisphere), and, for recognition of faces, for left hemifield presentations (right hemisphere). For field-dependent individuals, no significant differences can be observed between the two hemifields for either type of stimulus, and a tendency can be seen, even if slight, for a more rapid response for both letters and faces in right hemifield presentations. These results are compatible with the hypothesis of differentiation, which predicts that field dependence-independence is correlated with degree of functional segregation in the two hemispheres, more than with a general tendency to use one or the other hemisphere. The low correlation observed between performance level (reaction times) and field dependence confirms that these results cannot be confused with performance level per se.

Only male subjects were used in the experiment just described. However, Rizzolatti and Buchtel (1977), replicating the experiment on perception of faces in two samples of women, were unable to demonstrate the left visual hemifield superiority repeatedly seen in males for this task. The same authors also reported a similar pattern of results for the recognition of letters. In a subsequent experiment, Pizzamiglio and Zoccolotti (1981) attempted to study the differential influence of the sex factor and the field dependence factor on these two tasks. In this study, they selected two groups of equally very field-independent subjects (one male and one female) and two groups of equally very field-dependent subjects (one male and one female). There was no difference among the four cognitive groups in a test of verbal comprehension (Thurstone & Thurstone, 1947).

The results indicated that both male and female field-independent subjects showed a very marked right hemifield superiority for letter recognition and left hemifield superiority for the recognition of faces. However, more field-dependent subjects of both sexes showed minor, although significant, differences between the two hemifields for both tasks.

Whereas both cognitive groups favored the right visual hemifield for letter recognition, a difference in the direction, as well as in the importance of the effect, was also observed between the two groups for face recognition. Field independent subjects responded more rapidly to left visual hemifield stimuli, whereas more field-dependent subjects showed greater rapidity in the opposite hemifield, indicating a mediation of the left hemisphere for face recognition in more field-dependent subjects.

The latter result was also described in research carried out by Rapaczynski and Ehrlichman (1979). In this study, very field-dependent and very field-independent female subjects were presented with a unilateral task of face recognition in which the stimuli were presented in normal and upside-down positions. When the faces were upside-down, no lateralization effect occurred. But, for the normal orientation, the more independent subjects responded more rapidly and with less errors in the left hemifield; the opposite was true for more field-dependent subjects. However, there were no differences in degree of lateralization between field-dependent and field-independent subjects. It must also be noted that the task used (recognition of 7 faces out of 14) was particularly difficult for subjects producing RTs at around 1500 msec. It seems probable that such long reaction times are relatively unreliable and do not allow for the identification of differences in degree of lateralization.

In other research, the relationship between field dependence and a lateralized task of visual stimuli recognition in the presence of different coding instructions was studied (Longoni, Zoccolotti, & Speranza, 1980). First, the subjects were shown two words with high image content for 5 sec, then a figure representing one of the two words or a completely different object appeared for 100 msec to the left or to the right of the fixation point. The subject's task consisted of pressing one of two keys in the shortest possible time. In the absence of coding instructions, higher RTs occurred in this task for stimuli in the right visual field, which seems to indicate a prevalent linguistic coding of the stimuli. However, by using interactive imagination instructions, where the subject was asked to represent in a single mental image the objects corresponding to the two-word stimulus, Seamon and Gazzaniga (1973) encountered more rapid RTs in the left visual field indicating a mediation of the right hemisphere. In the sample studied by Longoni et al. (1980), a significant left visual hemifield superiority for the imagination condition was present only for more field-independent subjects, as measured by the RFT, whereas more dependent subjects showed a very small and insignificant tendency to favor the right hemifield. It is interesting that there was no difference in lateralization when the subjects were divided at the mean in a questionnaire of "imaginative vividness," modified by Betts into a daydreaming scale (Singer & Antrobus, 1972), or into a test of verbal fluency (Thurstone & Thurstone, 1947).

DISCUSSION

The presentation of this research makes possible the study of individual differences in the functional organization of the CNS, beginning with cognitive behavior measurements that are able to describe some characteristics of psychological functioning.

It has been shown that: (a) field dependence-independence represents a way of placing individuals along an information-processing continuum; (b) this description of individual differences is stable and, therefore, capable of characterizing prevalent modalities of individual functioning; (c) this psychological dimension is conditioned, in part, by biological regulation mechanisms; and (d) it is a good indicator of the degree of differentiation of the psychic system in general. Therefore, the general hypothesis has been formulated that individuals who differ from one another in psychological organization present diversity in greater and lesser specialization of functions between the two cerebral hemispheres.

This concept is compatible with empirical data indicating how cognitively more differentiated individuals (more field independent) tend to show more marked lateralization effects than do less differentiated individuals. In particular, this relationship has been found in the acoustic, tactile, and visual modality for tasks mediated by one and by the other hemisphere. Also, the relationship between psychological and neurological specialization cannot be traced back to a simple consequence.

The hypothesis formulated up to now does not predict a priori any directionality of lateralization effects. However, in experiments on tachistoscopic recognition of faces, opposite hemispheric effects have been evidenced for field dependent-independent subjects, which seem to indicate the adoption of different hemispheric strategies for solving the task. In terms of psychological differentiation, one might suppose that in the absence of a high degree of functional segregation in the two hemispheres and thus of the specialized modality for analyzing particular stimuli, the same analysis can be achieved by means of more general response mechanisms.

In the case of face recognition, Carey and Diamond (1977) described an ontogenetic tendency to pass from a feature-by-feature analysis, which takes into account particularly so-called paraphernalia (dress, eye glasses, beard, etc.) to a defined, configurational analysis, which takes into account the more complex aspects of the single physionomy. In particular, the authors observed that children from 6 to 8 years of age recognize an equal number of upside-down faces and faces oriented normally, while 10-year-old children tend to recognize faces oriented normally better than those turned upside-down. The behavior of the older children seems due to an increased capacity to process information in a configurational way. In fact, the 180° inversion of a face does not prejudice the possibility of analyzing single details but modifies completely the complex physionomy. Thus, it can be hypothesized that for more field-dependent subjects there may be a developmental delay for face recognition involving the existence of a preferential strategy for carrying out this task, based on the analysis of details, and that this is linked to left hemisphere prevalence. More field-independent subjects would use, instead, a more configurational strategy, mediated by the right hemisphere.

An important aspect of this hypothesis seems to be providing a unified frame of reference for the prediction of response patterns to lateralized stimuli.

A certain number of individual variations have been described in the literature (for example, sex and manual dominance) that influence in a consistent way interhemispheric organization (Harris, 1977; Varney & Benton, 1975). A verification of this requires that predictable variations on the basis of, for example, sex or manual dominance, be substantially referrable to variations in psychological differentiation. Results that are in agreement with this hypothesis can be found in the study by Pizzamiglio and Zoccolotti (1981). Using lateralized presentation of letters and faces, they clearly documented that the expected differences between males and females are entirely explainable in terms of different samples of field dependent-independent individuals of the two sexes. Thus, women show less marked lateralization effects in that they tend to be more field dependent, and the opposite occurs for men. This interaction between sex and field dependence in predicting effects of lateralization seems much more important because, as already stated, differences between men and women do not seem to be determined only culturally, but also through a transmission mechanism mediated by the X chromosome (Goodenough et al, 1977).

The discussion of anatomic differences in the literature suggests the possibility of describing individual differences (for example, in different functional recovery from aphasic disturbances) in terms of structural diversity. Where confirmed, the general nature of the relationship between differentiation at the psychological level and interhemispheric specialization can provide a more adequate and comprehensive conceptual instrument for awareness of these differences in the heretofore studied variables. In particular, sex and manual dominance, which up to now have received the greatest interest, do not seem able, due to their dichotomous nature, to exhaust the range of interhemispheric difference described at the anatomic level.

Certainly it is becoming increasingly more interesting to make use of research methodologies that confront more directly the problem of brain-behavior relationships, e.g., comparing data on the behavioral characteristics of the individual with anatomic reports relative to CNS functioning. The authors know of long-term research projects that are moving in this direction, but not of data available with respect to this problem.

REFERENCES

Axelrod, S., & Cohen, L. D. (1961). Senescence and embedded-figures performance in vision and touch. *Perception and Motor Skills, 12,* 283–288.

Benton, A. L., Varney, N. R., & Hamsher, K. S. (1978). Lateral differences in tactile directional perception. *Neuropsychologia, 16,* 109–114.

Bock, R. D., & Kolakowski, D. (1973). Further evidence of sex-linked major gene influence on human spatial visualizing ability. *American Journal of Human Genetics, 2* 1–14.

Carey, D., & Diamond, R. (1977). From piecemeal to configurational representation of faces. *Science, 195,* 312–313.

Connolly, C. J. (1950). *External morphology of the primate brain*. Springfield, IL: C. C. Thomas.

Corah, N. L. (1965). Differentiation in children and their parents. *Journal of Personality, 33*, 300–308.

Cunningham, D. J. (1892). *Contribution to the surface anatomy of cerebral hemispheres*. Dublin: Royal Irish Academy.

Duncker, K. (1945). On Problem Solving. (L. S. Lees, Trans.) *Psychological Monographs, 58* (5) (Whole No. 270).

Ekstrom, R. N., French, J. W., Harman, H. H., & Dermen, D. (1976). Manual for kit of factor-referenced cognitive tests. Princeton, NJ: Educational Testing Service.

Geschwind, N., & Levitsky, W. (1968). Human brain: Left-right asymmetries in temporal speech region. *Science, 461*, 186–187.

Gilbert, C., & Bakan, P. (1973). Visual asymmetry in perception of faces. *Neuropsychologia, II*, 355, 362.

Goodenough, D. R., Gandini, F., Olkin, I., Pizzamiglio, D., Thayer, D., & Witkin, H. A. (1977). A study of X chromosome linkage with field dependence and spatial visualization. *Behavior Genetics, 7*, 373–387.

Goodenough, D., & Karp, S. A. (1961). Field dependence and intellectual functioning. *Journal of Abnormal and Social Psychology, 63*, 241–246.

Harris, L. J. (1977). Sex differences in spatial ability: Possible environmental, genetic and neurological factors. In M. Kinsbourne (Ed.), *Hemispheric asymmetries of function*. Cambridge: Cambridge University Press.

Hartlage, L. C. (1970). Sex-linked inheritance of spatial ability. *Perceptual and Motor Skills, 31*, 610.

Hecaen, M., & Ajuiriaguerra, J. (1964). Left handedness. NY: Grune & Stratton.

Hounsfield, G., Ambrose, J., Perry, J., & Bridges, C. (1973). Computerized transverse axial scanning. *British Journal of Radiology, 46*, 1016–1015.

Inglessis, M. (1919). Einiges über Seitenventrikel und Hirnschwellung. *Archiv fuer psychiatrie und Nerven Krunkheiten, 74*, 159–168.

Karp, S. A. (1963). Field dependence and overcoming embeddedness. *Journal of Consulting Psychology, 27*, 294–302.

Kimura, D. (1967). Functional asymmetry of the brain in dichotic listening. *Cortex, 3*, 163–178.

Kuhn, G. M. (1973). The phi coefficient as an index of ear differences in dichotic listening. *Cortex, 9*, 450–457.

LeMay M., & Culebras, A. (1972). Human brain morphologic differences in the hemispheres demonstratable by carotid angiography. *New England Journal of Medicine, 287*, 169–170.

Lemay, M., & Geschwind, N. (1978). Asymmetries of the human cerebral hemisphere. In A. Caramazza & E. Zurif (Eds.), *Language acquisition and language breakdown*. Baltimore, MD: Johns Hopkins University Press.

Longoni, A., Zoccolotti, P., & Speranza, T. (1980). Coding strategies and hemispheric lateralization effects — a replication of Seamon and Gazzaniga. *Archivio di Psicologia, Neurologia e Psichiatria, 41*, 479–481.

Luria, A. R. (1972). *Traumatic aphasia*. The Hague: Monton.

McRae, D. L., Braunch, C. L. & Milner, B. (1968). The occipital horns and cerebral dominance. *Neurology, 18*, 95–98.

Mickle, W. J. (1898). Atypical and unusual brain-forms, especially in relation to mental status: A study of brain surface morphology. *Journal of Mental Science, 44*, 17–45.

Oltman, P. K., Ehrlichman, H., & Cox, P. W. (1977). Field independence and laterality in the perception of faces. *Perceptual and Motor Skills, 45*, 255–260.

Palmer, R. D. (1964). Development of a differentiated handedness, *Psychological Bulletin, 62*, 257–272.

Pizzamiglio, L. (1974). Handedness, ear-preference and field dependence. *Perceptual and Motor Skills, 38,* 700–702.

Pizzamiglio, L., & Carli, R. (1973). Caratteristiche psicometriche di alcuni test di dipendenza indipendenza dal campo. *Archivio di Psicologia, Neurologia e Psichiatria, 34,* 276–286.

Pizzamiglio, L., & Zoccolotti, P. (1981). Sex and cognitive influence on visual hemifield superiority for face and letter recognition. *Cortex, 17,* 215–226.

Pfeifer, R. A. (1936). Pathologic der Horstrahlung und der Corticalon Horsphare. In O. Bunke & O. Foerster (Eds.), *Handbuch der Neurologie* (6th Ed.). Berlin: Springer.

Rapaczynski, W., & Ehrlichman, H. (1979). Opposite hemifield superiorities in face recognition as a function of cognitive style. *Neuropsychologia, 17,* 645–652.

Rizzolatti, G., & Buchtel, H. A. (1977). Hemispheric superiority in reaction times to faces: Sex differences. *Cortex, 13,* 300–305.

Rizzolatti, G., Umilta, D., & Berlucchi, G. (1971). Opposite superiorities of the right and left cerebral hemispheres in discriminative reaction time to physiognomical and alphabetical material. *Brain, 94,* 431–442.

Rubens, A. B. (1977). Anatomical asymmetries of human cerebral cortex. In S. Harnad, R.W. Doty, L. Goldstein, J. Yanes, & G. Krauthamer (Eds.), *Lateralization in the nervous system.* NY: Academic Press.

Rubens, A. G., Mahowald, M., & Hutton, T. (1976). Asymmetry of lateral fissures in man. *Neurology, 26/7,* 620–640.

Seamon, J. G., & Gazzaniga, M. S. (1973). Loading strategies and cerebral laterality effects. *Cognitive Psychology, 5,* 245–256.

Serra, A., Pizzamiglio, L., Boari, A., & Spera, R. (1978). A comparative study of cognitive traits in human sex chromosome aneceploids and sterile and fertile enploids. *Behavior Genetics, 8,* 143–154.

Silverman, A. J., Adevai, G., & McGough, W. E. (1966). Some relationships between handedness and perception. *Journal of Psychosomatic Research, 10,* 151–158.

Singer, J. L.,, & Antrobus, J. S. (1972). Day dreaming, imaginal processes and personality: A normative study. In P. W. Sheenhan (Ed.), *The function and nature of imagery.* NY: Academic Press.

Stafford, R. E. (1961). Sex differences in spatial visualization as evidence of sex-linked inheritance. *Perceptual and Motor Skills, 13,* 428–435.

Teszner, D., Tzavaras, A., Gruner, J., & Hecaen, H. (1972). L'asymétre droite-gauche du planum temporale. A propos de l'étude anatomique de 100 cerveaux. *Revue Neurologique, 126,* 444–445.

Thurstone, C. L., & Thurstone, T. G. (1947). *Primary mental abilities.* Chicago: Science Research Associates.

Varney, N. R., & Benton, A. L. (1975). Tactile perception of direction in relation to handedness and familial handedness. *Neuropsychologia, 13,* 449–454.

Waber, D. P. (1976). Sex differences in cognition: A function of maturation rate? *Science, 192,* 572–573.

Wada, J. (1969). Interhemispheric sparing and shift of the cerebral speech function. *Excerpts Medica, International Congress Series, 193,* 296–297.

Wada, J., Clarke, R., & Hamm, A. (1975). Cerebral hemispheric asymmetry in humans. *Archives of Neurology, 32,* 239–246.

Whitaker, H. A., & Selnes, O. A. (1976). Anatomic variation in the cortex: Individual differences and the problem of the localization of language functions. *Annals of New York Academy of Science, 280,* 844–854.

White, B. W. (1954). Visual and auditory closure. *Journal of Experimental Psychology, 48,* 234–240.

Wilder, B. G. (1889). The brain anatomy. In A. M. Buck (Ed.), *A reference handbook of the medical sciences. Vol. 8.* NY: W. Wood.

Witelson, S. F., & Pallie, W. (1973). Left hemisphere specialization for language in the newborn: Neuroanatomical evidence of asymmetry. *Brain, 96,* 641–646.

Witkin, H. A., Birnbaum, J., Lomonaco, S., Lehr, S., & Herman, J. L. (1968). Cognitive patterning in congenitally totally blind children. *Child Development, 39,* 767–786.

Witkin, H. A., Dyk, R. B., Faterson, H. F., Goodenough, D. R., & Karp, S. A. (1962). *Psychological differentiation.* NY: Wiley.

Witkin, H. A., & Goodenough, D. R. (1976). *Field dependence revisited,* (ETS-RB 76-39), Princeton, NJ: Educational Testing Service.

Witkin, H. A., Goodenough, D. R., & Karp, S. A. (1967). Stability of cognitive style from childhood to young adulthood. *Journal of Personality and Social Psychology, 7,* 291–300.

Witkin, H. A., Moore, C. A., Goodenough, D. R., & Cox, P. W. (1977). Field-dependent and field-independent cognitive style and their educational implication. *Review of Educational Research, 47,* 1–64.

Witkin, H. A., Oltman, P. K., Raskin, E., & Karp, S. A. (1971). *Manual for the Embedded Figures Tests.* Palo Alto, CA: Consulting Psychologists Press.

Zangwill, O. L. (1977). *Cerebral dominance and its relation to psycholoical function.* Edinburgh: Oliver & Boyd.

Zoccolotti, P. (1977). *Field dependence and patterns of cerebral lateralization.* Paper presented at the 48th meeting of the Eastern Psychological Association, Boston, MA.

Zoccolotti, P., & Oltman, P. K. (1978). Field dependence and lateralization of verbal and configurational processing. *Cortex, 14,* 155–163.

Zoccolotti, P., Passafiume, D., & Pizzamiglio, L. (1979). Hemispheric superiorities on a unilateral tactile test: Relationship to cognitive dimensions. *Perceptual and Motor Skills, 49,* 735–542.

5 Field Dependence, Personality Theory, and Clinical Research

Sheldon J. Korchin
University of California, Berkeley

When I was a student, a story was told about a visitor to a British university who came to hear a lecture on psychoanalysis but was uncertain whether he had come to the right lecture hall. He asked the professor and was told, gently but firmly, "No, here *intellection* is taught. *Affection* is down the hall and *volition* is in the next building." This was very much the state of psychology when Hy Witkin started his research on the perception of the upright. Few would have conceived then (and some still find it hard to believe) that the way people differ in such simple perceptual tasks could relate so importantly to so many aspects of personality, human development, social functioning, psychopathology, clinical intervention, neuropsychological processes, and cultural adaptation. It was Hy's genius and persistence that allowed him to discover field independence-dependence in the first place and to trace its many ramifications over the following years.

Although trained in the Gestalt tradition, with its emphasis on the objective organization of the stimulus field, Hy realized early the profound truth in Wilhelm Stern's classic dictum that there is *Keine Gestalt ohne Gestalter.* As one of a small group of psychologists in the late 1940s, Witkin pioneered a "new look" in perception, searching out ways in which individuals structure their perceptual worlds along personalistically meaningful lines. Unlike many of his contemporaries, however, he looked at *how* people perceive — the structure and processes involved — rather than *what* they perceive, the content of perception as it might reflect individual needs and personality. His concern was less with the effect of personality on perception than with personality through perception. There is little question but that field independence-dependence, the cognitive styles Witkin discovered, have been the most important and widely studied of the cognitive styles identified to date.

WITKIN'S PERSONALITY THEORY

Hy noted in one of his last contributions (1978) that field independence-dependence have these qualities: (a) they are *process variables,* describing ways of orienting and functioning, rather than success in attaining goals; (b) they are *pervasive* dimensions of individual functioning; (c) along with their pervasiveness, they account for self-consistency in behavior, which is predictable across situations; (d) they tend to be *stable* over time, which need not imply unchangeability; (e) they are *bipolar.* Field dependent people have competencies distinct from those of the field independent (one is not simply the absence of the other); and (f) the bipolarity also points to the fact that these constructs are *value neutral.* (Neither field independence nor field dependence is better or worse than the other.) Each pole has qualities that help people adapt under particular circumstances. The process, pervasiveness, self-consistency, and stability characteristics of field dependence-independence have been stressed over many years; noting the bipolar and value-neutral nature of these constructs is a more recent emphasis, which makes possible study of field independence-dependence as they relate to personal and social adaptation (Witkin, 1978). Hy's theory was extended to account for the evolving findings of recent years; these new trends also predict future development of the theory and new research directions.

Fundamentally, field-independent and field-dependent people are distinguished by their performance on simple perceptual and intellectual tasks. Field-dependent persons depend on external referents to achieve solutions; field-independent persons utilize internal referents. Over a wide range of procedures, the field independent show greater skills in cognitive restructuring and the field dependent greater interpersonal competencies. Field-independent persons are able to segregate and manipulate abstract concepts; field dependent persons are more at home with people, whom they need particularly in ambiguous situations to provide them with standards for judgment and action. It is no surprise, therefore, that field-independent students move toward fields such as mathematics and the sciences, whereas field-dependent students favor the humanities, social sciences, and human-helping professions. Similarly, over a wide variety of studies, field-independent people function more autonomously of others in a social situation; field-dependent people are more interdependent with others, although they are no more dependent in an emotional sense.[1]

---

[1]The statements in this paragraph, and much of the text that follows, are supported by numerous empirical studies. Rather than cite individually the many investigations relating field

Such differences between the field-dependent and the field-independent reflect the higher-order construct of *self-nonself segregation,* which in turn is a particular, though centrally important, aspect of the still higher construct of *psychological differentiation* (Witkin, Goodenough, & Oltman, 1979). A more differentiated person shows more self-nonself segregation; there are more definite and firmer boundaries "between an inner core of attitudes, feelings, and needs identified as the self, and the outer world, particularly other people" (p. 1127). As part of a more segregated self are a more articulated body concept and a greater sense of personal identity. Overall, the more segregated the self, the more likely a person is to be field independent, having greater cognitive restructuring skills though fewer interpersonal competencies. As Witkin's earlier studies showed (Witkin, et al., 1962), greater self-segregation (hence, autonomy, field independence, articulated body concept, etc.) seems to result from child rearing practices that emphasize gaining independence from parental controls.

Since 1962 the concept of differentiation has stood central in Hy's theory. As currently conceived (Witkin et al., 1979) differentiation can be viewed as standing at the apex of a conceptual pyramid, with its qualities being defined by lower-order constructs, as pictured in Fig. 5.1.

As noted, Self-nonself segregation is one facet of differentiation, represented by field-independence-dependence and revealed in the balance of Restructuring skills and Interpersonal competencies. Two other major expressions of differentiation are the Segregation of psychological functions (represented in more Structured controls and more Specialized defenses) and the Segregation of neurophysiological functions, as seen in hemispheric specialization. Thus, in its current conceptualization, differentiation stands at the top of a pyramid. The three next lower order constructs are Self-nonself segregation, Segregation of psychological functions, and Segregation of neurophysiological functioning. At the lowest level are such functions as restructuring skills and interpersonal competencies, structured controls and specialized defenses, and hemispheric lateralization, which have provided operationalized measures of the three mid-level constructs in numerous empirical studies.

With this new conceptual schema, Hy's theory becomes even more powerful as a framework for understanding personality and social functioning, within which the findings of literally thousands of studies can be integrated. Differentiation theory provides a powerful dimension along which behavior in numerous realms can be ordered and understood. As Hy noted, differenti-

---

dependence-independence to diverse aspects of psychological functioning, we refer the reader to the major books, monographs, and review articles published by Witkin and his associates and cited at the end of this paper (e.g., Witkin, 1965, 1978; Witkin, Dyk, Faterson, Goodenough & Karp, 1962; Witkin & Goodenough, 1976, 1977, 1981; Witkin, Lewis, Hertzman, Machover, Meissner, & Wapner, 1954).

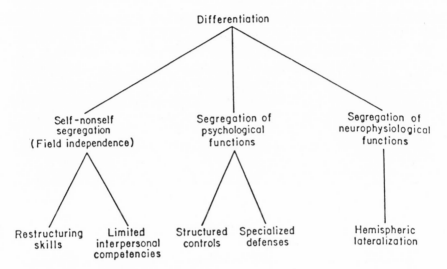

FIG. 5.1   Proposed differentiation model (1979) (Reproduced from Witkin, Good-enough, & Oltman, 1979).

ation deals more with the structure than with the content of experience, and only secondarily with its motivation. In Allport's terms, it looks at the nomothetic side of psychological life, examining people in terms of variables common to all, but not directly at the ideographic qualities that characterize particular individuals. That Hy was becoming more concerned with this issue is reflected in his sections on Individuality and Diversity in the Heinz Werner Lectures (Witkin, 1978), which I believe revealed as much his personal aversion to typologies and his profound commitment to a democratic ethos as the necessary trend in his theory. I also believe it is fair to summarize his position as arguing that differentiation theory does not deny personal uniqueness but neither does it focus on and try to explain it.

There are other loose ends in differentiation theory. Defining field independence-dependence as bipolar variables and value neutral did allow Hy and his colleagues to consider the adaptive value of each mode of functioning and to note the advantages and disadvantages of both. Yet the operational base for assessing field independence-dependence remains unidimensional, measures on which one performs better or worse, not differently. Lesser cognitive restructuring skills emerge as greater interpersonal skills, justified by a network of correlations but not directly assessed. The bipolar nature of field independence-dependence still needs to be demonstrated.

There is another issue worth considering. Over its long history, the consistency and stability of field independence-dependence were its most impressive features. Consequently, until recently, little attention was given to the conditions under which people's cognitive styles might change, either through life events or intentional interventions — this is the problem of fixity and mobility, as Hy phrased the issue in the Werner Lecturers (Witkin, 1978). That some people can function only in one mode, while others might move from one to the other, is a challenging hypothesis. But as yet we do not have sufficient guidelines, either conceptually or empirically, for predicting the circumstances in which these alternatives may occur. These issues remain for the future to resolve. That differentiation theory was incomplete, and itself constantly differentiating, was something that Hy understood well.

Looking broadly at Hy's contribution to personality theory, I am reminded of a story told about Robert Maynard Hutchins, who led the University of Chicago in its most glorious period. Someone once asked him, "Do you mean, Mr. Hutchins, that the University of Chicago is the best possible university?" To which Hutchins somewhat modestly replied, "Of course not. It is the not the *best possible* university — just the best there is!" And so it is with Hy's differentiation theory.

CONTRIBUTIONS TO CLINICAL PSYCHOLOGY

Controls and Defenses

We have seen that the differentiated person is characterized by more articulated controls and more specialized defenses. On the whole, field-independent people have been found to be less impulsive and direct in the expression of affects, both as children and adults, in a variety of studies using behavioral observation, projective tests, and experimental tests. Compared to the field-dependent, among the field-independent affect expression is more modulated and controlled. Similarly, in studies of motor inhibition, which require subjects to perform a simple and familiar action as slowly as possible — for example, writing one's own name or walking a straight line — field-independent people are better able to inhibit and control their behavior. Findings of this sort have generally emerged from studies of children, although in some cases observational studies have failed to find the expected relation between field independence and impulse control. As one might predict, however, hyperactive children are characteristically field-dependent. Therefore, field-independent people may be said to have more structured controls and be better able to regulate emotional discharge and to control motor activities.

With more structured controls go more specialized defenses. Numerous studies employing many methodologies converge on the generalization that defenses used predominantly by field-independent and those used by field-dependent people differ systematically. The field-independent favor isolation, intellectualization, and projection; field-dependent people, on the other hand, are more likely to use denial and repression, as evidenced in the Rorschach and other projective techniques, studies of clinical interviews and therapeutic interaction, and on the Gleser and Ihilevich Defense Mechanism Inventory, among other procedures. Relevant, but less direct, evidence has emerged in experimental stress studies. Field-dependent subjects are more affected by stressful material in perception and are more apt to forget previously learned stressful (as compared to neutral) material. Similarly, people who tend to forget their dreams, particularly if stressful, are more commonly found to be field dependent. The overall theme of this body of research is clear — The more field-independent, differentiated person uses defenses that are more differentiated and more advanced developmentally, such as intellectualization and isolation. Such defenses are more congruent with the more abstract and conceptual orientation of the field-independent person, for they serve to protect the integrity of the intellectual processes against the intrusion of potentially disturbing affects. Field-dependent persons have fewer conceptual resources to utilize such defenses and do not have as great a need to segregate intellectual from affective life because of their dominantly interpersonal rather than impersonal orientation.

However, as Hy insisted, the use of more or less specialized defenses need not imply greater or lesser mental health or psychological adjustment. Each type of defense can be used adaptively or maladaptively, serving coping or neurotic needs. The overuse of any mechanism leads to pathological solutions to life problems, particularly if used extensively, repeatedly, and inappropriately. Intellectualization can protect cognitive functioning from unwanted emotional distraction. At the extreme, however, it separates thought processes from the enriching influence of affect. By similar logic, repression and denial more common to the field-dependent person can have more adaptive or more pathological consequences. What is clear is that field-independent and field-dependent people favor different defenses, in ways predictable from differentiation theory; that one or the other type of defense is better or worse, does not follow from this fact.

Psychopathology

That field independence-dependence is not a simple correlate of mental health is clear in Hy's analysis of their relation to psychopathology. Early in their work, Hy and his colleagues found that among the patients of a psychiatric hospital many were extremely field dependent, and many were extremely field independent. It became clear that field dependence-independence did not predict whether a person would be mentally ill or healthy, or the extent of pathology, but rather the form pathology would take, if present. As predicted from the theory of the time, depressed patients were found to be more field dependent, while field-independent patients were more likely to be paranoid. This finding paralleled the fact that women, usually more field dependent, tend toward depression; men, relatively more field independent, tend toward paranoid symptoms.

Supportive findings emerged in a study I conducted with Romulo Rossi, Franco Giberti, and other colleagues of the Clinica delle Mallatie Nervose e Mentali of the Universitá di Genova in 1960. To test the differentiation hypothesis, we divided all incoming patients into five groups, ranging from, at one extreme, those who expressed their pathology primarily in somatic terms, who were depressed, or who showed more diffuse symptoms, to the other extreme, patients with more articulated symptoms, obsessional neurotics, and paranoid schizophrenics. On the Embedded Figures Test, these groups went from greater field dependence (somatizers and depressed patients) to greater field independence (obsessional and paranoid patients).

By the time of his 1965 review (Witkin, 1965), Hy reported a large network of relations among many clinical phenomena and field dependence-independence. Patients with problems of dependency, who are likely to lack a sense of separate identity, are more commonly field dependent. Thus, alcoholics, obese people, ulcer patients, and asthmatic patients are found to be more field dependent. Hallucinatory patients are more field dependent; those with delusions, more field independent. Persons with hysterical rather than obsessional defenses, those who turn aggression inward instead of outward, those more prone to shame than guilt, are all more usually field dependent. So too, patients with character disorders, those who somatize their problems, and those who act out rather than contain affect expression also tend to be field dependent. At the other extreme, patients who have delusions and ideas of grandeur, who direct aggression outward, and who continue to struggle to maintain identity, however bizarre, are more field independent. Such patients include obsessive-compulsive characters, paranoids, and relatively well-organized ambulatory schizophrenics, among others. In the 15 years since the 1965 paper on "Psychological Differentiation and Forms of Psychopathology", a growing literature supports and extends the earlier findings, as Lewis (1980) recently showed.

Hy argued consistently that field-independence-dependence relates to the form but does not predict the presence or the extent of pathology. What type of symptoms a person might develop can be predicted from his level of differentiation. On what does the presence and extent of pathology depend? To answer this question, Hy (Witkin, 1965) calls attention to the twin constructs of differentiation and integration. *Differentiation* refers to the complexity of structure of a psychological system. A major quality of a differentiated system is specialization of function; another is the segregation of self from nonself. By contrast, *integration* refers mainly to the form of the functional relations of the parts within the system and the system as a whole with its surroundings. At any level of differentiation, different modes of integration are possible. In Hy's view, adjustment is mainly a function of the effectiveness of integration; that is, the more or less harmonious working together of the parts of the system and of the system as a whole in relation to its environment. Deficiencies in integration account for psychopathology, which can occur with any degree of differentiation. Thus far, the determinants of integration still remain to be discovered. However, the large body of work on differentiation and psychopathology contributes importantly to the old but still unresolved question of "symptom choice" — why people dysfunction in particular ways when they can no longer cope adequately.

DIFFERENTIATION AND PSYCHOTHERAPY

Theory and research on field independence-dependence have also contributed to our understanding of psychotherapy and, more generally, psychological change.

Field-dependent people, we might predict, are less likely to seek out psychotherapy in the first instance. Being less psychologically minded, and more likely to somatize or deny their problems, the "talking cure" may seem less relevant to them. When they do come to clinics, they are less apt to be welcomed by psychotherapists. Studies show that clinicians are more likely to recommend supportive rather than modifying or exploratory treatment, preferring to have the client worked within a more structured than an unstructured situation. Field-dependent patients, on their part, seek guidance rather than insight in the therapeutic encounter. It is interesting to note that different therapeutic roles go along with differences in differentiation of therapist. Thus, Pollack and Kiev (1963) found that extremely field-independent psychiatrists favored either a directive-instructional role or a passive-observational approach, whereas relatively more field-dependent colleagues leaned toward more personal and mutual relations with their patients.

Interesting findings are emerging from matching studies. A sizeable literature on social interaction suggests that people matched in cognitive style are more likely than mismatched people to develop interpersonal attraction, in the context of psychotherapy as well as other forms of social interplay (Oltman, 1980). Thus, college roommates who had similar cognitive styles were more satisfied with the arrangement than those who were dissimilar in style. More patients treated by therapists who differed from them in cognitive style dropped out of therapy by the end of two months, compared to patients treated by therapists who shared their cognitive style. In matched pairs, patients expressed greater satisfaction with their treatment. The greater affinity of matched pairs appears in nonverbal as well as verbal behavior. More eye contact has been reported between partners in matched dyads, although there was no difference overall in the amount of eye contact made by field-independent and field-dependent people. These findings parallel the findings of Michael Smith (1979) who worked with me on the behavior of black subjects interacting with black or white interviewers; there was more eye contact and also more satisfaction expressed in the black-black pairs. People matched in cognitive style, or other important characteristics, feel more comfortable with each other. This does not necessarily mean, however, that therapy will be more effective, even though it may be easier to relate initially to someone similar to oneself. The purpose of therapy is not simply to enjoy being with one's therapist; its purpose is to change the patient in significant ways, which may in fact be facilitated by differences between the two participants. However, as my colleague Enrico Jones (1978) has shown in racial matching studies, differences in important cognitive or social qualities are significant, particularly in the early stage of psychotherapy and must be seriously considered in planning psychological interventions with those who may differ from us.

If we now look more closely at the process of therapy, many interesting findings related to cognitive style emerge. Witkin, Lewis, and Weil (1968) studied patients through the first twenty sessions of psychotherapy. Each participating therapist was assigned one highly differentiated and one relatively undifferentiated patient, without knowing which was which. Therapists made decidedly more comments to the less differentiated than to the more differentiated patients (about three times as many in the first session). Some less differentiated patients made only brief replies that required more questions to get the desired information. Others, however, were in an excited state, saying a great deal, but in repetitive, disorganized bursts, which also required the therapist to make many specific comments in order to guide the flow. On the other hand, differentiated patients often came to the first session with a well-developed and organized account of their problems and beliefs as to their causes, whether correct or not. Sometimes they gave the impression of having a prepared statement. Because of such behaviors, these therapists entered few comments into the therapeutic transaction. A number of other qualities distinguished the behavior of less differentiated patients, some of which increased the number of comments they made; they often agreed with the therapist or repeated part of his statement; they solicited support ("Is that normal, doctor?"); they attempted to prolong the hour because of separation anxiety.

Later studies have shown that field-dependent patients tend to reveal more of themselves in therapy sessions and as interviewees during an interview. Field-dependent people score higher on Jourard's Self-Disclosure Questionnaire. Ancona and Carli (1971) found that field-dependent subjects showed more emotional involvement in the events of a film they had just watched. Although some of these findings are not specific to the therapy process, they, along with the less articulated, more dependent, and guidance-seeking behaviors noted by Witkin, Lewis, and Weil (1968) in their study of therapy process, suggest greater self-disclosure and emotional involvement among the field-dependent.

But, does cognitive style have anything to do with the outcome of therapy? This, after all, is our ultimate concern as clinicians. Here the findings are fewer, and we can only speculate. In his 1965 analysis (Witkin, 1965), Hy noted that two questions can be put: 1) Does field-independence-dependence itself change as a result of therapy? and 2) Are field-independent or field-dependent people more likely to change in beneficial ways as a result of therapy? On the first question, Hy (Witkin, 1965) expressed doubt that field independence-dependence could itself change. He pointed to the evidences of stability to be found both in longitudinal studies and in the generally unsuccessful efforts to produce change through experimental interventions. However, in a more recent reconceptualization of the issue (Witkin, 1978; Witkin & Goodenough, 1977), Hy considered the possibility of inducing change more seriously. Thus, in *Field Dependence Revisited* (1976), the authors state: "Training in personal autonomy, as through therapy, would, according to our hierarchical model, contribute to increased skill in cognitive restructuring, even though therapy does not concern itself directly with improvement in that domain" (p. 28).

In answer to the second question—Does field independence-dependence relate to therapy outcome in terms of better adjustment or greater mental health?—Hy ventured a couple of hypotheses. The first was that patients with greater mobility would likely do better than those who were more fixed in cognitive style. Specifically, he predicted that people who are relatively differentiated and, at the same time, more mobile, that is, able to move toward more or less differentiated functioning as situations require, would be best able to gain from therapy. The second hypothesis was that people in the mid-ranges, rather than those at either extreme, would gain more, because they seemed to be more mobile as well.

Clearly, there is much research to do in this area. However, one fact is clear. Field dependence-independence is a potentially important variable in the study of both therapy process and outcome, for it relates to the ways people transmit and process information, adapt or malfunction in life situations, express and resolve their problems, and relate to each other, in therapy as in other human relations. In earlier days of psychotherapy research, when only the simple question was asked—Does it work?—a concept of such importance in distinguishing different types of human functioning may have been less relevant. But, as psychotherapy research has become more subtle and differentiated, the question has evolved into: What kind of people, treated by what kind of therapist, with which mode of therapy, under what circumstances, change in what respects? Such questions require far more subtle analyses, within which consideration of field independence-dependence can have an important role. Perhaps matching therapist and patient is important; existing data suggest this. Perhaps therapeutic interventions and process ought to be altered to serve the needs of each group better. The possibility that differentiation itself can be changed through intentional intervention, as well as through the generic processes of therapy, makes the quest more challenging.

CONCLUSION

I share with Hy Witkin the faith that neither the field-independent nor the field-dependent person is any more or less human (though they do differ), neither is any more or less likely to suffer human problems (though the problems may differ), nor is one or the other any less deserving of help (though the nature of the help offered may have to differ).

Differentiation theory evolved and, indeed, differentiated over the years, and will continue to do so into the future, even without Hy's genius to guide its growth. The ideas speak for themselves and should continue to challenge us to extend, amplify, and, if necessary, change them.

As in any body of work, there are some conceptual inconsistencies, many unresolved issues, and gaps in our knowledge. Some of these I have called attention to; others have been discussed in the literature. His dear friend and long-time collaborator, Helen Block Lewis (1980), has questioned a fundamental premise by asking: "Why *must* cognitive restructuring and interpersonal skills be negatively related?" If we remember the man himself, the wisdom of her question becomes clearer. The concepts of his theory seem limited when applied to Hy Witkin himself.

The pleasure with which Hy Witkin could manipulate abstract constructs in manifestly diverse realms reveals the highest order of restructuring ability, of the sort that characterizes the most field-independent person. As in Herbert Spencer's definition of genius, Hy could make the homogeneous heterogeneous and make the heterogeneous homogeneous. Yet, along with this preeminently field-independent cognitive style, Hy was an intensely human, empathic, and loving man. He had a profound interest in people and deep affection for them, as all of us whose lives he touched know so well.

REFERENCES

Ancona, L., & Carli, R. (1971). The dynamics of cinematographic participation. *Ikon, 76,* 47–73.

Jones, E. E. (1978). The effects of race on psychotherapy process and outcome: An exploratory investigation. *Psychotherapy: Theory, Research, Practice, 15,* 226–236.

Lewis, H. B. (1980). *Clinical implications of field dependence.* Presented in the H. A. Witkin Memorial Symposium, Eastern Psychological Association.

Oltman, P. K. (1980). *Psychological differentiation theory in social and cross-cultural psychology.* Presented in the H. A. Witkin Memorial Symposium, Eastern Psychological Association.

Pollack, I. W., & Kiev, A. (1963). Spatial orientation and psychotherapy: An experimental study of perception. *Journal of Nervous and Mental Disease, 137,* 93–97.

Smith, M. (1979). The effects of cross-racial matching on nonverbal behavior in psychological interviews. Unpublished doctoral dissertation, University of California, Berkeley.

Witkin, H. A. (1965). Psychological differentiation and forms of pathology. *Journal of Abnormal Psychology, 70,* 317–336.

Witkin, H. A. (1978). *Cognitive styles in personal and cultural adaptation.* 1977 Heinz Werner Lecture. Worcester, MA: Clark University Press.

Witkin, H. A., Dyk, R. B., Faterson, H. F., Goodenough, D. R., & Karp, S. A. (1974). *Psychological differentiation.* Potomac, MD: Lawrence Erlbaum Associates. (Originally published 1962).

Witkin, H. A., & Goodenough, D. R. (1976). *Field-dependence revisited.* Princeton, N.J.: Educational Testing Service.

Witkin, H. A., & Goodenough, D. R. (1977). Field-dependence and interpersonal behavior. *Psychological Bulletin, 84,* 661–689.

Witkin, H. A., & Goodenough, D. R. (1981). *Cognitive styles: Essence and origins. Field dependence and field independence.* New York: International Universities Press.

Witkin, H. A., Goodenough, D. R., & Oltman, P. K. (1979). Psychological differentiation: Current status. *Journal of Personality and Social Psychology, 37,* 1127–1145.

Witkin, H. A., Lewis, H. B., & Weil, E. (1968). Affective reactions and patient-therapist interactions among more differentiated and less differentiated patients early in therapy. *Journal of Nervous and Mental Disease, 146,* 193–208.

Witkin, H. A., Lewis, H. B., Hertzman, M., Machover, K., & Meissner, P. B., & Wapner, S. (1972). *Personality through perception.* Westport, CT: Greenwood Press. (Originally published 1954).

6 Clinical Implications of Field Dependence

Helen Block Lewis
Yale University

One of my most vivid recollections of Hy is of him wondering—indeed, marvelling—at how it could be that the number of degrees off the true upright at which a stick was seen as straight in a tilted frame, could predict so much else about a person. The wide-ranging network of correlations that can be put together meaningfully with field dependence as a focus, is reflected in the works of this volume. The network of connections literally touches all areas of psychology—from cerebral hemisphere localization to obedience in agrarian versus hunter-gatherer ecologies—including shame and guilt. The network of connections to field dependence boggles the mind not only by its breadth but because one glimpses the promise of profound advances in the field of psychology with the advancing theoretical integration of the network.

Hy's discovery during the 40s that a pervasive, self-consistent style of perceiving is associated with personality style was a first step along a road that he then courageously pursued. I say courageously because the intellectual climate in the 40s was not particularly friendly to a concept of perceptual style, let alone one that would reflect personality. It is instructive to remember just how "way out" most of psychology in the 40s regarded the notion of connecting perceptual and personality styles. The concept of a self that might be a center for both was not available either in Freudian theory or in behaviorist thinking. At one edge of academia, workers in the Freudian tradition were showing how orally and anally fixated characters were playing out their childhood experiences in their adult personalities. Orally satisfied infants, for example, were shown to be optimistic, if somewhat self-indulgent, adults (Goldman-Eisler, 1951). Similarly, Fromm (1947) showed us how the orderly, obstinate, and parsimonious qualities of the anal character were essential for men living in a mechanized, competitive, industrial society. This was all evidence, however, of how childhood personality style might issue in a similar adult personality style. It did not directly support a view that connected perceptual style with personality style.

At another edge of academia, Freudian-influenced experimenters were trying to trace perceptual distortions to conflictual states (e.g., Postman, Bruner, & McGinnies, 1948) but with mixed success since the phenomena being studied were so ephemeral both on the affective and the perceptual sides. In a revisionist Freudian movement, psychoanalysts following the lead of Hartmann (1951) were theorizing about a conflict-free, autonomous as opposed to an id-based ego. This concept suggested, for example, that a wide range of noxious experiences in childhood would still permit ego functions to develop at appropriate times. But such a view was really quite close to that of mainstream academic psychologists, who had always taken it for granted that motivational and emotional states had little to do with perception. Within academia the issues were, rather, whether perceptual functioning was better predicted by Gestalt or S-R formulations. Hy's discovery occurred as he, in collaboration with Asch, was pursuing conflicting evidence about Wertheimer's predictions as to the influence of the framework on the perception of the self's position in space (Asch & Witkin, 1948a, 1948b). That an individual might bring with him into the Gestalt something of his own personality was quite unpredicted and initially very difficult to comprehend. The judgment that it was important to pursue personality styles as a determinant of performance within the Gestalt cognitive context was Hy's alone.

When Hy first suggested to me that he could guess performance on the Rod-and-Frame Test from meeting and talking with his subjects, and that I should try to guess from a clinical interview who would tend to line up the stick with the frame, I wondered on what basis such a guess could ever be made. I remember sitting with Dorothy Dinnerstein, who was an observer at those pilot interviews, giggling nervously about how certain we would sometimes be about our predictions simply on the basis of whether the person had impressed us as having a strong, not to say disagreeable self, or else a more accommodating and compliant self. The guessing game worked remarkably well and Hy's determination to pursue the problem of "how come" was reflected in the title of his first book: *Personality through Perception* (Witkin et al., 1954).

With hindsight one can now see that field dependence has become so powerful a tool because it catches the self as it organizes to respond to its surround. It can thus be used as a "tracer element" (the term Hy liked) to pursue the self's relation to the nonself, as this intersects both personality formation and cognitive development. In my own view, this theoretical task would be facilitated if a distinction were made between two meanings of the nonself: first, the self's relation to the nonself in the sense of the inanimate or physical world; and, second, in relation to emotionally significant others. These two areas of the nonself make very different demands on the organization of the self. In emotional relationships, the boundaries between the self and the other are necessarily fluid: what affects the other person also affects the self in empathetic and vicarious experiences. At one emotional extreme, early difficulty in making a satisfactory attachment to others may express itself in withdrawal from them into a substitute or symbolic attachment or interest in the physical world. This is a pattern that has been described, for example, for autistic boys (Mahler, Pine, & Bergman, 1975). Such a preoccupation with inanimate objects in space could foster development of a field-independent cognitive style through emotional deficit. In another pattern, such as has been described for symbiotic girls (Mahler et al., 1975), difficulty in separating the self from significant others may be expressed in an inability to bear separation from mother and in an almost total neglect of interest in the physical world. Such a pattern would foster field-dependence by another kind of emotional default. Still another pattern of stable emotional attachment would presumably predict a self both interpersonally adept and field-independent.

In the current status of differentiation theory (Witkin, Goodenough, & Oltman, 1979), there is the paradox that restructuring skills and limited interpersonal skills are both seen as outgrowths of self-nonself segregation or field independence. In this view, ". . . the greater recourse of field-dependent people to external referents [meaning, in this case, others], stimulates the development of interpersonal competences but may be responsible for these people's lesser cognitive restructuring skills. Relatively field-dependent and field-independent people may be seen as making their main developmental investment in different domains" (p. 1139).

What this theoretical formulation leaves unsolved, however, is why there should be an inverse relationship between social skills and cognitive restructuring skills, why the two differing domains of emotional and cognitive development should not proceed in a positive rather than a negative interaction. Why should women's ability to judge the warmth of other people's feelings go together with difficulty in cognitive restructuring? (Rapaczynski, Welkowitz, & Sadd, 1979). I do not have the answer to this problem, but I do suggest that a distinction between the self as it organizes its attachment to others and the self as it organizes its relation to inanimate objects is useful in positing a two-track self-nonself segregation that begins the process of differentiation. It seems likely, and there is some evidence, that the two tracks begin by interacting positively (Kogan, 1976). They may stop doing so when socialization processes begin to require more cognitive skills from one gender and more interpersonal skills from the other.

In any case, the importance of field dependence in targeting clinical problems was apparent from the beginning of the work, when a psychiatric hospital population turned in a surprising number of both extremely field-dependent and extremely field-independent performances. It was early apparent that field dependence is related not to the extent of pathology but to its form. As intuitively predicted at the time, depressed patients were more likely to be field-dependent, while paranoid patients were more likely to be field-independent. This difference clearly paralleled the propensity of women to be more prone to depression (a fact not so well known then as it has since become), and the corresponding propensity of men to become paranoid. By the time of the 1965 paper (Witkin, 1965) on differentiation and forms of pathology, an enormous network of clinical connections existed with field dependence at its center: alcoholism, obesity, ulcers, hysterical versus obsessional defenses, repression versus isolation of affect, turning aggression against the self versus outward, shame versus guilt, suitability of patients for psychotherapy, and the quality of the patient-therapist interaction, to name just a few connections. In the 20 years since the publication of that paper, the accumulated evidence has strengthened the validity of clinical predictions that can be made from field-dependence.

Let me cite just a few good studies. On the question of depression, Levenson and Neuringer (1974), using suicide as the ultimate criterion of depression, predicted and found that male suicides had significantly lower scores on the performance triad of the WAIS (Object-Assembly, Picture-Completion and Block-Design) than a comparable group of psychiatric patients. The authors describe suicides in cognitive style terms, as persons lacking the "problem-solving processes to re-orient [their] relationship to [their] environment" (p. 184). Cognitive formulations of mental illness are more fashionable today than those on the affective side, and this, in my opinion, is one-sided. But I console myself at once with the recollection that the field-dependence construct can make the bridge to an equally appropriate formulation that describes suicides as unable to separate themselves from significant others.

On the corresponding question of paranoia, a dissertation completed at Yale (Johnson, 1980) predicted and found that paranoid schizophrenics (mostly male, as usual) were significantly more field independent than a comparable group of nonparanoid schizophrenics.

A study (Seif & Atkins, 1979) of phobic patients is particularly instructive. A distinction was made between animal phobias and situation phobias (commonly called agoraphobias) on the basis, in part, of their differing phenomenologies. Animal phobics are characteristically hypervigilant as to the stimulus evoking their dread. The spider phobic, for example, is an expert in locating the spider at the periphery of his vision — it "pops out" of context into his awareness. For situation phobias, in contrast, the phobic stimulus is less specific. The appearance of phobic response, moreover, is heavily influenced by the prevailing context, varying in intensity with differing contexts.

On the basis of this analysis, Seif and Atkins predicted and confirmed that animal phobics would be more field independent than situation phobics. They also predicted and found that animal phobics are significantly more often given to intellectualization, whereas situation phobics are given to repression and denial. This is an important finding with implications for therapy; we know that more animal than situation phobics respond well to systematic desensitization, perhaps experiencing the no-nonsense, business-like, impersonal approach of behavior modification as more sympathetic to their emotional style.

My own corner of this clinical garden has flourished since I began to focus on guilt and shame as these grisly states affect peoples' vulnerability to psychiatric symptoms (Lewis, 1971). The immediate network on which I concentrate has shame, depression, hysteria, and female gender connected to field dependence; with guilt, obsessional and paranoid symptoms, male gender, and field independence in a corresponding package. Evidence is needed at all points in this package. A significant linkage has been found (Smith, 1972) between depression and proneness to shame, with the association being particularly strong for women. A recent study (Crouppen, 1977) of normal and depressed males found field dependence to be an excellent indicator of proneness to shame, but an earlier study of normals (Schubert, 1974) failed to obtain any relationship. Colby's (1977) work on the computer-simulated paranoid interview suggests that inability to bear shame is the main factor propelling paranoids to project guilt.

The focus on shame and guilt is fruitful because it catches people in the complicated cognitive and affective states by means of which they maintain their attachment to significant others. Shame and guilt are differing modes of organizing the self to ward off the loss of attachment. Shame is directly about the self in relation to others, guilt is more about things or events in the world. If one followed the lead of field dependence in studying situation versus animal phobias, one could predict that situation phobics are more prone to the subjective and indefinable experiences of shame vis-à-vis others, whereas animal phobics should be more prone to the objective and specifiable experiences of guilt. This is a testable set of hypotheses. Another testable hypothesis is that situation phobics might be better off in therapy with a relatively field-dependent therapist.

As this work was being prepared, I kept remembering the criteria Hy set for appraising work. There are two that I found most salient. The first is the great importance of what questions one asks—what lines of inquiry are opened up. The second is the extent to which one has stimulated others to answer questions that raise more questions. By both criteria, Hy's contribution to psychology has been enormous, and I find it a comfort that its full magnitude will surely be appreciated far into the future.

REFERENCES

Asch, S. E., & Witkin, H. A. (1948a). Studies in space orientation: I. Perception of the upright with displaced visual fields. *Journal of Experimental Psychology, 38,* 325–337.

Asch, S. E., & Witkin, H. A. (1948b). Studies in space orientation: II. Perception of the upright with displaced visual fields and with body tilted. *Journal of Experimental Psychology, 38,* 455–477.

Colby, K. M. (1977). Appraisal of four psychological theories of paranoid phenomena. *Journal of Abnormal Psychology, 86,* 54–59.

Crouppen, G. (1977). Field dependence-independence in depressed and normal males, as an indicator of relative proneness to shame or guilt and ego functioning. *Dissertation Abstracts, 37,* p. 4669.

Fromm, E. (1947). Psychoanalytic characterology and its application to the understanding of culture. In S. Sargent & M. Smith (Eds.), *Culture and personality.* New York: Viking Fund.

Goldman-Eisler, F. (1951). The problem of "orality" and its origins in early childhood. *Journal of Mental Science, 97,* 765–782.

Hartmann, H. (1951). Ego psychology and the problem of adaptation. In D. Rapaport (Ed.), *Organization and pathology of thought.* New York: Columbia University Press.

Johnson, D. (1980). *Cognitive organization in paranoid and non-paranoid schizophrenics.* Unpublished doctoral dissertation. Yale University.

Kogan, N. (1976). *Cognitive style in infancy and early childhood.* Hillsdale, NJ: Lawrence Erlbaum Associates.

Levenson, M., & Neuringer, C. (1974). Suicide and field dependency. *Omega, 5,* 181–186.

Lewis, H. B. (1971). *Shame and guilt in neurosis.* New York: International Universities Press.

Mahler, M., Pine, F., & Bergman, A. (1975). *The psychological birth of the human infant.* New York: Basic Books.

Postman, L., Bruner, J., & McGinnies, E. (1948). Personal values as selective factors in perception. *Journal of Abnormal and Social Psychology, 43,* 142–154.

Rapaczynski, W., Welkowitz, J., & Sadd, S. (1979). Affect judgment and field dependence. (ETS RR 79-5). Princeton, NJ: Educational Testing Service.

Schubert, C. (1974). *Embedded figures performance on an indicator of relative proneness to shame and guilt.* Unpublished doctoral dissertation, Texas Agriculture & Mining University.

Seif, M., & Atkins, A. (1979). Some defensive and cognitive aspects of phobia. *Journal of Abnormal Psychology, 88,* 42–51.

Smith, R. (1972). *The relative proneness to shame or guilt as an indicator of defensive style.* Unpublished doctoral dissertation. Northwestern University.

Witkin, H. (1965). Psychological differentiation and forms, pathology. *Journal of Abnormal Psychology, 70,* 317–336.

Witkin, H. A., Goodenough, D. R., & Oltman, P. K. (1979). Psychological differentiation: Current status. *Journal of Personality and Social Psychology, 37,* 1127–1145.

Witkin, H. A., Lewis, H. B., Hertzman, M., Machover, K. Meissner, P. B., & Wapner, S. (1954). *Personality through perception.* New York: Harper & Row. 2nd Edition, (1972). Westport, CT: Greenwood Press.

7 Implications of Field Dependence for Social Psychology

Renzo Carli, Franco Lancia, Rosa Maria Paniccia
University of Rome

THE PSYCHO-SOCIAL COMPONENTS OF
PSYCHOLOGICAL DIFFERENTIATION

In discussing the implications of field dependence for social psychology, we will begin by describing the psychosocial dimensions present in the theory of psychological differentiation. We emphasize that our purpose is not to dissect Witkin's theory with the aim of pulling out only those aspects pertinent to social psychology. Such a procedure would fractionate a theoretical construct whose heuristic value, originality, and current validity are principally found in the formulated hypotheses taken as a whole, in their experimentally-proven connections. Our objective is an ambitious one: By singling out the psycho-social components of the model and reconsidering them critically, we propose to show that the theory of psychological differentiation is, if considered from a particular point-of-view, a psycho-sociological theory.

We begin with a description of the model: theoretical constructs, according to Goodenough and Witkin (1977), are hierarchically ordered within a pyramidal structure similar to that found in factorial analysis models. *Differentiation,* located at the apex, is defined as the most relevant formal property of an organismic system. Accordingly, a little-differentiated system presents a state of relative homogeneity, whereas a more-differentiated system occurs in a state of relative heterogeneity.

We believe, as do Witkin, Goodenough and Oltman (1979), that level of differentiation is largely an organismic function. The hypothesis at the basis of this assumption is that every tendency of the individual to function in a more or less differentiated way has the probability of being manifested through psychological and neurophysiological activities. It follows that modes of functioning and behaviors identified as demonstrations of higher differentiation or indicators of lower differentiation have high probability of becoming manifest in relationship to each other.

The theoretical formulation under analysis includes three major differentiation indicators: the separation between psychological functions, between self and nonself, and between neurophysiological functions. These indicators are seen across specific modes of functioning and behaviors. The first (separation of psychological functions) is manifested through structured controls and specialized defense mechanisms. The second (separation between self and nonself) allows for greater autonomy in confrontation with environmental stimuli and goes back to the construct of cognitive style, that is, field dependence-independence. Within the area of differential individual behavior, the hypothesis is accepted that field-dependent subjects have greater probability of developing competence in interpersonal relationships as a function of their more extended utilization of external referents, which can be understood as relationships with others during the course of development. In contrast, field-independent subjects carry out behaviors characterized by greater ability in cognitive restructuring, due to their greater autonomy in confrontation with the immediate perceptual field when the information processing originating from it must be utilized to respond to situational demands or internal needs. The third indicator (separation of neurophysiological functions) becomes concrete in a specialization, through lateralization, of the cerebral functions that are seen, under the psychological profile, in the separation between affect on one side, and ideas and perceptions on the other.

Up to this point the only dimension that directly relates to social psychology is interpersonal competence, a behavioral manifestation characterizing field-dependent subjects who are endowed with less functional autonomy and less differentiation between self and nonself.

A second reference specific to psycho-social dimensions is encountered when factors that may influence the development of differentiation are analyzed. Many cross-cultural studies have clearly demonstrated the influence of socialization on functional autonomy. Social structures that encourage young people and children to adopt autonomous attitudes and behaviors in confrontation with parental authority and the social structure to which they belong tend to produce persons who show a more striking tendency toward field independence. The contrary is true within social structures that encourage or induce an attitude of conformity with respect to authority.

Further affirmations of psycho-social relevance emerge from the theoretical construct under analysis when ecocultural factors of adjustment, which have been found in studies carried out on social groups of so-called primitive cultures (i.e., microsocieties functioning at the survival level with different modalities and adjustment strategies), are taken into consideration. In particular, nomad groups who base their survival on hunting, as well as sedentary groups who base their survival on rudimentary agricultural activities have been studied. The first cultural structure seems to produce field-independent individuals, whereas the second cultural structure produces field dependent individuals. These studies allow for the postulation of a direct relationship between the different adjustment demands presented to individuals belonging to one or the other of these contrasting ecological structures and the development of their cognitive styles during the course of ontogenesis.

Goodenough and Witkin (1977) affirm that these findings can also be understood as indirect proof of the probable progression that has accompanied and characterized cultural development throughout human history from primordial to most recent times, from a relatively field-independent cognitive style to a relatively field-dependent one.

A final point regarding psycho-social relevance concerns the experimentally verified hypotheses regarding the influence of social adjustment models, recognized as being relevant in different cultures, on the development of differentiation between self and nonself, and thus on the functional autonomy and cognitive style of its members. Using Pelto's (1968) polarized classification of social structures, which distinguishes a tightness and a looseness in different social contexts, it is noted that tight societies, with complex international structures and where there is strong pressure toward conformity to different authority figures expressed through considerable role differentiation, are characterized by field-dependent persons. The contrary is found in looser societies, which are less structurally complex, less differentiated in the roles assigned to or assumed by their members, more tolerant of personal initiative, and thus less responsive to norms.

As we have seen, a unique psycho-social dimension seems to be present within the differentiation model. This involves competence in interpersonal relations, generally accepted as characterizing field-dependent subjects whose low differentiation between self and nonself involves greater trust in external referents and thus a greater connection with others within the adjustment process.

Moreover, socialization is analyzed as a factor that may influence in relevant ways the differentiation process during development. Socialization may utilize parameters of cultural induction, including pressure to conform to authority and to the differentiation and specialization demands of social roles; encouragement or tolerance of autonomous attitudes toward authority. This process of socialization is based not only on role adequacy but also on more correct strategies to achieve the organizational objectives.

These findings may seem more pertinent to educational psychology than to psycho-sociology. This is not so if we delve more deeply into the psycho-sociological implications that the model of differentiation offers as a whole.

However, before launching into this analysis, it is important to point out a further finding regarding the neutral value that the bipolar dimension of the field dependence-independence variable evidences. According to Witkin and Goodenough (1977), this signifies that both poles, between which cognitive style is articulated, have adjustment valence.

This assertion disproves the widespread tendency to consider cognitive style under a value profile such as "Field independents are better than field dependents." This may be significant for the psycho-sociologist who, on the basis of interest and competence, has a strong probability of being field dependent! This finding allows for a re-reading of the entire model, with a view toward considering the intervention of the different constitutive variables within the social adjustment process so as to single out the psycho-dynamic origins of the social link. In particular, it would be interesting to consider, as the initial element of analysis, the opposition between restructuring ability and interpersonal ability or competence. This involves the psychological manifestations of a differentiation indicator that appear fundamentally relevant in the sphere of social adjustment. Is it possible to consider three dimensions within the unitary socialization model? And, moreover, is it possible to trace back to the same model the behavioral manifestations of the other two indicators of differentiation considered? We believe that it is possible to respond to these questions by reconsidering the process of social adjustment in its complex articulation and by singling out from it the fundamental component.

ORGANIZATION AND INSTITUTION

We introduce the socialization model by distinguishing between two aspects of social interaction, which will then be considered in terms of their relation and reciprocal influence.

Social interaction may be defined as the modality across which human beings pursue transformative-type goals necessary for survival of the individual and the species. Transformation (Carli, 1976) is understood as the action of the social group directed toward carrying out change regarding a particular environmental context, from an initial state A to a terminal and planned state B, in order to constitute this context as object and to allow for its development and cultural, historical and social management.

Therefore, at the basis of the transformation process is the planning act, limited by the mediation of symbolic thought that allows for the categorization of environmental stimuli as events and of behavioral responses as actions. The planning of the terminal state shapes the latter as the model to which the transformative action must adjust itself to guarantee the linearity of the change from the initial to the terminal state, planned and predefined in its connotations. Hence, the transformative process may be considered as a model-discard type structure, expressed during the three planning moments of the tightly interdependent action and evaluation. Evaluation, in particular, takes shape as the result of the discarding between the model and the outcome of the transformative action. This signifies that, according to a pragmatic profile, every different outcome of B (terminal outcome) is evaluated for its non-B connotation, for its difference from or discarding of B. The transformative system has its own pragmatic effectiveness in the planned definition of the terminal state and in the corrective intervention of the discardings with respect to it. As Beretta (1974) affirms:

> In the case of man it seems that nature has adopted a completely original solution directive in order to achieve a biological system with high adjustment potential among a wide gamut of environmental conditions: i.e., a complex of interactive structures no longer uniquely predetermined by genetic patrimony, but ever available for a morphogenetic modeling, within certain reversible limits, on the part of the current stimulation. (p. 34)

Social organization, in this view, involves cognitive psychological study for the analysis of responses to the environment that the organism processes on the basis of incoming information. In particular, transformative organization postulates a *consensus* of its members on the objectives pursued, a parceling out of the functions assumed by individuals and by groups within the transformative dynamic, and the acceptance of shared norms that regulate the process.

There is question regarding the psychodynamic model on which the consensus is founded that is fundamental for the organization and its functioning. The classical theory of organization, in its different articulations, has responded to this question by postulating the *rationality* of the structure based, in turn, on the economic motivation that characterizes its members. But an attentive reading of social reality shows a high probability of encountering disaffirmations of the organizational rationality pretext, pointing out conflicts, deceptions, paradoxal, and unforeseen outcomes. Just when one would expect the most compact rationality, the most irrational dynamics emerge.

One can also note that not all that emerges in the realm of social structure can be traced back to organizational reality. There is frequent manifestation of relational dynamics that do not appear in relation to what is postulated by transformative interaction and yet which assume particular relevance within the structure.

The psychoanalytic model seems to offer several theoretical findings, which, if correctly extended to the dynamics of social relations, can account for this phenomenology that crosses organizations and conditions functioning and that we call "institution." We will describe it in its genetic process in order to draw out useful indications for an intervention. It is that phenomenology which constitutes the specific object of the investigation and of the psychosociological praxis.

Psychoanalytical theory and research have evidenced drive duplicity as a human characteristic and as fundamental for individual and species survival because it promotes the development of the friend-enemy schema of symbolization in the adjustment process controlling correct behavioral decisions in confrontation with environmental events. Moreover, the existence of a life drive and a death drive (libido and destrudo) poses several important problems concerning the control of aggression in social relationships. The problems presented by the human being's drive duplicity are considered here. In the animal species, the control of intraspecies aggression is regulated by genetically determined mechanisms, time controlled by the intervention of binomial mutation-selection.

Using the Kleinian theory (Klein, 1948) as reference, let us consider how the regulation of drives in the mother-child relationship is carried out. We take care to consider not only the interpsychic dynamic but also the relational dynamic that characterize that relationship. The mother-child relationship may be considered as the first demonstration of the prolonged neotenia situation, that is, a deferred dependency relationship of the newborn on parental care that, as generally affirmed, constitutes the element characterizing the adjustment of the human species to the environment. This precocious mother-child relationship demonstrates the univocalness of the object-mother and its gratifying (and thus positive) connotation in comparison with the drive duplicity motivating and orienting the child's attitude. A fundamental and decisive problem is thus posed regarding reciprocity: the child could, in fact, cathect the mother, good-object, with positive affect, whereas the child could not know where to polarize the destructive drive. In this regard, it must be remembered that, for Klein (1948), drives must find an object right from the beginning of life since "the experience of an instinct in the mental apparatus is linked with the phantasy of an object adjusted to the instinct" (Segal, 1968, p. 16).

To avoid the anguish of annihilation, provoked by a cathexis of the death drive on the self, the child deflects the death drive onto an external object. In this way, the object becomes evil and persecuting, thus allowing for the conversion of a part of the drive itself into aggression. According to Segal (1968), the original fear of the death instinct is changed into fear of a persecutor. But onto which object is the death instinct deflected? The child does not have a multiplicity of objects at its disposal. Therefore, it uses the mother, the only object available, modeling the drive cathexis on the absence-presence of the object itself. The child experiences objects only as absent or present. If the object is present it becomes a good object; if it is absent it becomes a bad object. This symbolic duplicity may parallel the drive duplicity that characterizes the child's affective experience.

If the mother is able to bear the attacks directed toward her by the child, if she knows how to take on the blame and give him back, attenuated, the persecuting anguish of which she is the object, through amending behavior the child will be able progressively to base his drives inside himself and acquire that trust in an internal good object, founded on libidinal supremacy, which is so important for subsequent development.

Let us consider for a moment the particular situation in the mother-child relationship when the latter separates the object and the mother responds with depressed or reparational behavior that attenuates the persecution anguish of the child. A first finding concerns the mental processes put into action by the child. This involves a scission of the unique object, based on its presence or absence. Moreover, what emerges from the scission is symbolized by the child in terms of ideal object with which to test a relationship of positive univocal reciprocity, and in terms of persecutor object with which to carry out a relationship of negative reciprocity. Scission and symbolization denote the characteristics of the phantasmic processes, with clear affective valence, in the measure in which they are directed toward a reclamation of the relationships, toward a solution of the anguishing ambivalence, toward an institution of reciprocity.

Now we come to the mother's response. Her acceptance of blame and the attenuated restitution of anguish through reparational initiatives appear to be based on two distinguishing elements of the relationship: the unreal danger of the attacks directed toward her by the child, based, in turn, on the child's real dependence on her; that is, the hypothesis of the reversibility of the dependency itself, or, stated another way, the mutant valence which must necessarily compensate the mother's reparational initiatives and their effectiveness. The latter connotation is a specification of the former. If the child is unable to emancipate himself from the dependence, the tie that unites him to his mother necessarily becomes frustrating for her and, thus, truly threatening. The two conditions outlined, together with the processes of reciprocal interaction between mother and child, constitute an instituted relationship model that we define as *dual institution*.

Within the limits of the evolutive process it is possible to single out other instituted relationship structures, which we call *triadic institution* and *tetradic institution*. The former occurs in the relationship between the child and the parental couple. As in the dual institution, the scission, with the consequent phantasmic presence of the idealized and persecutor object, has the aim of structuring a phantasmically formulated relationship model so as to guarantee the reciprocity relation. The scission occurs inside the relationship between the parents, with the idealization of one of the two figures and the persecuting symbolization of the other. Characterizing this institutional dynamic is the negation of the sexuality represented by the couple, as difference generating and as limit to the infantile situation. In this way, a fusional relation is structured with the idealized figure, accompanied by the simultaneous negation of the other figure, perceived as limiting and normative.

The tetradic institution takes place in the relationship between child couple, on one side, and parental couple, on the other. The scission occurs along the axis of the generational relationship, with the aim of encouraging a positive reciprocity, also lived on the phantasmic plane and based on a process of affective symbolization within the relationship between children. At the same time, a negative reciprocity is favored between the latter and the adult subgroup. What characterizes this institutional dynamic can be described as idealization of innovative and counterdependent values of the youth culture, in contrast with values of permanence and conservation stereotypically associated with the adult dimension and symbolized as persecuting to guarantee reciprocity.

Heretofore, a too tight synthesis of the relational vicissitudes brought into action by the child within the complex family relationship has been formulated. The hypothesis we intend to propose concerns the institution of reciprocity within the realm of organizational structures as well. What has emerged from our research allows for the definition of *institution* as the reproduction, among the different components of the organization, of unconscious relational modalities borrowed symbolically by the dual, triadic, or tetradic institutions, and finalized by instituting the reciprocity relationship within the organizational relation.

Thus, social structures present a double level that may be analyzed: under an organizational profile these are characterized by the transformative objectives and are then articulated in relationships between persons oriented by the role and by the function carried out, regulated by implicit or explicit, formal or informal norms.

On the other hand, within them is the problem of the control of aggression, control necessary for the adequate functioning of the structure itself. To this end, collusive-type relationships are established. They are founded on the unconscious assumption of phantasmic images directed by the process of affective symbolization, which reproduce the relational modalities brought into action in the family realm and which are established to provide a stable solution to the control of aggression through the institution of reciprocity. For example, school, if considered from an organizational viewpoint, can be completely described as social structure directed toward fostering the learning experience. In this sense, it can be analyzed by means of the components of functioning that characterize it: programming, didactics, and evaluation. These components are necessarily based on the relationship between teacher and students and thus carry a social significance. Programming, for example, cannot involve only the ministerial program regarding a specific discipline, but must also be founded on an analysis of the demand of the pupils, their expectations, and the "initial" state that they present to the teacher and to the group in which the learning process will take place. Without this preliminary analysis, in which the teacher and the pupils must participate in their respective roles, the operation of programming risks being deprived of its significance and becoming an empty ceremony of accomplishment to a directive whose goals are unclear. Analogous considerations may be brought out also for didactics, for evaluation, and for the ties that place these three aspects of organizational functioning in strict interdependence.

Thus, a whole series of manifestations and relational conventions that may be singled out of school experience, but that do not seem to be part of the whole of structural characteristics required by organizational functioning, would not be comprehensible in a strictly organizational analysis. In fact, what significance can be placed on discipline within a structure delegated to produce learning? Why, for example, is interaction with the teacher accepted and considered "good discipline," whereas that between pupils is discouraged and punished? In a recent study of report card evaluation (there was a recent change in the Italian school system from numerical evaluation to a written assessment of the student), 52% of the affirmations made by teachers had to do with the disciplined behavior of the pupils, whereas only 19% referred to the acquisition of skills and knowledge, which is the aim of schooling (Lo Cascio et al., 1979). This finding becomes understandable if we consider the institutional dynamic implicit in school interaction. Teachers and pupils tend to institute a dual-type relational dynamic, where discipline is the manifestation of conditions of unreal danger for the child and learning signifies the expression of the reversibility of dependence. These two conditions allow for scission, by the pupil, of the teacher-figure into the two idealized and yet persecuting components, and the reparational function of the latter through the action of teaching.

In this briefly described example concerning school structure, many other aspects of institutional phenomenology could be explored to show how the dual institution, described in its reparational aspect, can, in particular situations, assume a persecuting or deforming modality (Kaës, 1973).

It is also interesting to note the possibility, utilizing particular criteria of social structure analyses, of showing an institutional phenomenology next to an organizational one. This point, however, still seems incomplete. In fact, it places institution and organization "next to" each other. Little is changed by affirming "institution through organization" or using other metaphors that all seem to denounce the lack of a model within which the relation between organization and institution is located. In other words, we are dealing with the singling out of ties that were initially separated. This investigation appears particularly important if we consider that, based only on the knowledge that it allows for, it is possible to establish the sense of institutional analysis, thus psycho-sociological praxis.

SYMBOLIZATION AS LINK BETWEEN ORGANIZATION AND INSTITUTION

It has been stated that institution is definable as a collusive, phantasmic process of mutually affective symbolization between members of the social structure, directed toward establishing an unconscious order of the relation founded on reciprocity. Further, this involves asymmetrical reciprocity founded on dynamics that we may call pregenital, with reference to the psychoanalytic model of the development of sexuality. Reciprocity is carried out through a replay of family relations, transposed into the realm of organizational structure.

It has also been stated that the pursuit of reciprocity finishes with the control of aggression in the realm of social relations. More specifically, control of the aggression quota has not been tied by the libido in the bridling of the death drive, which Freud (1937) speaks of concerning the relationship between ego and drives in the process of individual adjustment. But how does this process occur in the social relationship, where it is not possible to postulate the removal or the fusion of the drives as dynamics in the control of aggression?

If we return to transformation, the constituent of the organizational moment, we can see that it is founded on planning, an eminently symbolic act. Now the symbolization process is examined from a psychodynamic viewpoint, as an event that overcomes the tight hermeneutic borders, where one thing stands for another on the basis of resemblance (metaphor) or contiguity (metonymy). Abraham (1978) showed that in symbolization an indirect representation is achieved that proposes a solution on the linguistic plane, which opposes doing-acting out of the ambivalence innate in the objective relationship symbolized. We believe that the symbol substitutes a desired and, at the same time, prohibited action with a discourse that satisfies both the desire and the prohibiting image. This occurs through a process of affective indetermination of the symbol and its subsequent re-determination, which confers on it a specific connotation, one of the many made possible by in-determination.

Thus, transformation as organized action directed toward the achievement of a symbolically-based plan can be understood as solution of the original, unconscious ambivalence in confrontation with the object. Only the libidinal drive is cathected on it as if there were not also the death attitude. On the other hand, to which organizational components does the desire of which we speak belong? It is not possible to give a univocal response to this question. It can be shown that, historically, transformation has entered into the areas of social power, rightly emphasized as relevant from the historical-materialist approach, that is, power implying the influence of one social group over another, exerted through binomial formation-repression (Carli, 1976) and manifesting explicitly the failure of an hypothesis of consensus on the objectives of the different components of organizational structure. Furthermore, this may occur at a much different level in historically evolving situations within which the different organizational contexts are located. Therefore, the institution of reciprocity allows for the control of aggression present in social relations but which has not been developed within transformative symbolization. Also with regard to institution, a dynamic of symbolization is spoken of, defined as affective. In this case we are dealing with a "symbolic equation" (Segal, 1957), where no difference is found between symbol and symbolized and a highly symmetrical operation (Matté Blanco, 1975) that follows the laws of functioning of the unconscious system.

In this sense, it also is possible to speak of complementariness between institutional and organizational dynamics. In other terms, the institutional area can be understood as the site where the drive quotas, which have not been channeled into achieving the desire and symbolically anchored to the object through the transformation, are developed.

NEW PERSPECTIVES FOR INSTITUTIONAL ANALYSIS

Now we can analyze the model of socialization in the light of what has been asserted by the theory of psychological differentiation. As the basic premise of our analysis we again emphasize the affirmation, presented previously, concerning the adjustment valence that both poles hold in the bipolar articulation of differentiation. In particular, we note that the declination of both poles of the differentiation indicators may, on one side, lead back to the organizational phenomenon and, on the other, to institutions. The differentiation indicators and their behavioral manifestations will be considered here not only in the perspective of individual differences, but also in terms of the function which the various articulations of differentiation may hold within the socialization process.

We have seen that organizational behavior, directed toward achieving a transformative object, is based on the consensus of the participating members of the organization itself, on functional and role aspects, and on the acceptance of the norms which regulate its functioning. At the basis of the consensus it is possible to single out the importance of the processes of structured control that preside over the establishment of interiorized values and defined models of behavior, as an important basis for the regulation of drive expressions and of drive energy in the realm of the transformative action. If, more-over, we consider the processes of symbolization and categorization that al-low for the exact planning action of the transformation process, we note that they are made possible by the intervention of specialized defenses, projection and isolation. We note as well the separation between ideas and thoughts, on one side, and affect on the other. This separation results in hemispheric dom-inance with functional lateralization as the outcome of the differentiation of neurophysiological functions.

The planning process, moreover, appears to be based on the ability to restructure the field within which one operates when required to do so by the transformation task, within the limits of the most varied perceptual and intel-lective activity. We must insert, within the sphere of organizational response, the inhibitory control action of the immediate activation of the effectors on the part of current stimulation, in favor of the intervention of a central medi-ation, suitable for planning transformative behavior. The selection capacity and oriented direction of the activated operative sequences have an organiza-tion as a sequence to subordinate actions in hierarchic order, at a high level of differentiation and integration. Thus, due to its effectiveness, the organizational level of the social action postulates the use of all of those di-mensions considered within the limits of the model of psychological differen-tiation that are located on the side of differentiated development.

An analogous consideration is possible also for the institutional compo-nent, which crosses social organizations. Moreover, in this case, the dimen-sions of the model that are found on the side of undifferentiation, appear to be fundamentally important. The symbolic equation that controls affective symbolization, instituted to guarantee reciprocity in the sphere of interaction is, in fact, based on the confusion between affect and ideas, as much as on the destructuralization of drive control and on the low differentiation between self and nonself, components that allow for the reproduction of primitive re-lational models of high asymmetrical reciprocity instituted in the sphere of social interaction.

The problem concerning adjustment valence of interpersonal compe-tencies is both complex and interesting. We know that, in situations of ambi-guity, field-dependent subjects show a higher utilization of external social referents that aid in the removal of the ambiguity (Witkin & Goodenough, 1977). Field-dependent subjects are more attentive to social stimuli. They in-dicate a preferential orientation toward interpersonal relationships, thus showing interest in others; they are emotionally open and prefer to act within social situations. We know also that the social institution is based on the pos-sibility of transposing already tested collusive relationship models in the sphere of relational structure, in order to achieve reciprocity. These opera-tions of transposition and collusion are achieved through an affective symbolization of the relational components characterizing the organizational dynamic. This affective symbolization, which serves to resolve, in terms of reciprocity, an ambiguity otherwise present in the relational sphere, is possible due to attention to the social dynamic and to those social stimuli that constitute the necessary referent for symbolization itself.

Therefore, the social structure, in its organization and institutional articulation, seems to involve specific modes of functioning and behavior which regard both the area of high and low psychological differentiation. On the other hand, this is within the social structure, as noted previously with regard to complementariness between organization and institution. This signifies that in conditions of stability and progress, the institutional dynamic tends to be highly automated, whereas the accent is placed on organizational functioning and the problems linked to it. Instead, institutional problems emerge with greater evidence in moments of social change when new structural or cultural aspects appear, and the problems presented by them cannot be confronted on an eminently transformative plane without a preliminary formulation of institutional reorganization.

We think that this perspective of an historical and social-dynamic reading of social structures is more useful than the structuralist models that seem to want to define specific social dimensions in absolute terms; in particular Pelto's (1968) classification of social structures within the bipolar continuum defined by the tight rigorousness or lax permissiveness of the dominant culture. The former can be understood as social structures that indicate a profound resistance to change and which, therefore, propose a strict defense of the current institutional order, whose permanence becomes the false objective of the structure that is substituted for all other transformative ends. For example, this is the case with school structures, which, in carrying out their goal of a disciplinary tutelage — that appears as the true and proper defense of the established institutional order or of the status quo — seem to have forgotten their transformative aim linked to the production of learning. The latter, on the contrary, seem more able to formulate in transformative terms change which has already been formulated through a stable institutional reorganization, thus encouraging creativity and initiative, that is, the operative symbolization of its members.

It can be asserted that these latter social structures may follow the former in a particular phase of cultural and structural evolution, but may then be found in the conditions described as paradigmatic for the first category — in a later historical moment and as a function of a contingency — which various factors may produce.

It must be remembered that the study of these particular social structures is primarily, if not exclusively, oriented toward the analysis of the "product" in terms of differentiation, that is, toward the verification of field dependence or field independence characterizing the individuals who test their evolutive socialization within these structures.

Therefore, in this type of research a view can be shown which is at the same time valuing and pedagogic: valuing because it seems to indicate a preference, even if expressed as problematic, for modalities of socialization that bring out the field independence of the subjects who participate in them; pedagogic because it indicates a method across which it can intervene to influence the process of differentiation, assimilated in this perspective in a learning dynamic. However, since the earliest writings on psychological differentiation as formal characteristics of a system (whether psychological, biological, or social) differentiation and integration have been indicated. Within the sphere of integration, the complexity, indicating the level of development of the relations between components of the system and of the same with the environment, and effectiveness, has been emphasized. This is defined as follows: "To say that integration is effective signifies that there is a reciprocal more or less harmonious working of the components of the system and of the total system with its environment, so as to contribute to the adjustment of the organism." (Witkin et al., 1962, p. 26).

If by this organism we mean (and this is our view) an individual or a social group, we may see how adjustment (unique discriminator that allows for the validation of a model through the inevitable confrontation with reality) may result from interactions between more or less differentiated components, each able to carry out a particular role within the limits of the same process of adjustment. These interactions, integrated and directed toward adjustment may, on the other hand, appear to be different when the historically located social organism indicates different modalities of relation between its organizational and institutional components or when the social group is found in different positions in confrontation with the problem posed by the change.

We think that it is possible to suggest and plan a different investigative perspective that involves overthrowing the terms with which the psychological differentiation model has been utilized in social research. It involves not only verifying the potential of social systems to induce specific cognitive styles in their members, but also the experimental study of the effectiveness on the organization and institutional levels, which the presence of more or less differentiated behaviors assume, and the analysis of the interaction at the end of the process of change.

This study is already the object of psycho-sociological praxis, but in this sphere a heuristic category is lacking within which to place the behavior of the individual components of the group and their interaction. We believe that for our purposes the complex, yet simple, concept Herman Witkin developed may serve as an invaluable aid.

EXPERIMENTAL RESEARCH

The results that have emerged in several studies on school adjustment and learning processes are here presented to demonstrate the implications of differentiation and, in particular, of cognitive style, for the school dynamic.

The first experimental situation was as follows: 20 elementary school teachers (4th and 5th grade) were asked to indicate which pupils they would judge as maladjusted and to complete their report with an equal number of children who were the best adjusted to the school situation.

The use of the maladjustment-adjustment criterion to construct the sample was justified on the basis of analyzing the cognitive and social adjustment structures in subjects who were notable for their more or less elevated adjustment to the norms and value systems of their teacher (which, therefore, condition the school experience). The analysis of the factors used by the teachers for reporting purposes, and identified during a semistructured interview showed a prevalence for the dimensions involving learning, interest in school activity, and disciplinary behavior (in that order).

The hypothesis was that maladjustment-adjustment was resolvable in the incongruency between the learning norms communicated by the teachers, which were undifferentiated and thus inadequate in several cases to encourage the learning process and the development of cultural stimuli, and the learning strategies that would have to be presented in a different way for individual pupils as a function of their basic ability.

The hypothesis can be stated as follows: (a)   The maladjusted are less endowed than the adjusted, according to an intellective profile. This assertion is justified on the basis of the reported criteria adopted by the teachers. But this characteristic as an hypothesis does not exhaust the situation distinguishing children as maladjusted. The latter phenomenology can be correctly interpreted also on the basis of the hypothesis that follows:

(b)   In the initial phases of the learning process the maladjusted individual would be able to utilize an exploratory-type strategy, whereas the adjusted individual would be able, from the first phase onward, to efficiently adopt an automated strategy.

The two strategies can be defined on the basis of the point on the axis of the abscissa where the decision-making criterion in situations of uncertainty is fixed as indicated by the Signal Detection Theory. On the basis of this theory, the performances of a subject, who decides in situations of uncertainty, are described by two independent factors, namely *sensitivity* (d'index) and *criterion* (beta index). The first is defined by the distance between the means of the two probability curves with which the noise is distributed, on one side, and the only signal to be singled out, on the other. The criterion, as stated previously, is represented by the point on the axis of the abscissa where the subjective values of probability of the two curves unfold, above which the subject responds affirmatively of the presence of the signal, to which he responds negatively.

A restricted criterion, characterizing an automated strategy, is located at the high values of the probability distribution and corresponds to a strategy of singling out the signal based on the greater security that the signal is present in the observation interval. An enlarged criterion of the exploratory strategy is found against the low values and corresponds to a strategy of singling out the signal, which assumes the risk of a false alarm error, that is, of finding the signal in the presence of the noise alone, with the end of increasing the probability of singling out the signal itself.

The adequacy of one or the other strategy depends on the level of overlapping between the two distribution curves of the probabilities; the greater the overlapping of the two curves, the greater the decision-making uncertainty. In this case an automated strategy reduces the probability of need for false alarm errors and, at the same time, increases that of omission errors, thus reducing the probability of singling out the signal. The exploratory strategy, on the contrary, allows for the increase of the latter probability which is, moreover, paid with a strong increase in false alarm errors.

In the measure in which the area of overlapping between two curves is reduced, the automated strategy that allows for the singling out of the signal, maintaining the rate of false alarm and omission errors at a low level, appears more adequate. Therefore, it is evident that the exploratory strategy appears more adequate in the initial phases of the learning process; this could, then involve a more automated strategy.

The norm transmitted by the teachers in the school culture guarantees the adoption of automated strategies, independent of the initial position of the subjects in the learning sphere, since the errors found and associated with significant costs in the sphere of school experience of the culture of the country in which it exists and in which the experiment is carried out, are generally those of false alarm. Thus, the hypothesis is that there are no differences in the strategies utilized by adjusted and by maladjusted subjects, and that the common strategy is of the automated type.

In particular, the adoption of this strategy on the part of the adjusted subjects occurs on the basis of their ability to cognitively structure the decision-making situation; that is, in singling out the more adequate categories of analysis for finding the signal in situations of uncertainty, on the basis of their effective discrimination between signal and noise. For the maladjusted, on the contrary, the adoption of the automated strategy, inadequate for their cognitive performance, is hypothesized as being based on the adherence to the culturally-induced norm in school experience.

(c) The maladjusted subjects, who adopt an inadequate strategy on the basis of social pressure, do so as a result of being field dependent. The adjusted subjects, in contrast, are more field independent; their categorization in the decision denotes greater differentiation in the separation between self and nonself.

Used in this research were the following:

1. Embedded Figures Test (EFT)
   Acoustic Embedded Figures Test (AEFT) for measuring cognitive style.
2. Raven's Progressive Matrice 38 (PM 38) for measuring intellective level (d' index)
3. The measurement of the decision-making criterion was achieved through a specific reading of the data that emerged from the AEFT and the PM 38; the latter were modified from their original structure (Carli, Pizzamiglio, Scolari, 1974). Both trials were presented as decision-making tasks on the presence or absence of the signal in the single items considered as decision intervals where an evaluation of level of security that the subject entrusted to the rating method was requested.

In particular, the decision-making criterion was measured with the beta index, according to Hochaus's formula (1977).

C index was also calculated based on the application of the rating method, indicating the level of regularity in the variation of the criterion within the decision making categories suggested by the order of the two trials. The value of C index, a function of the variability of the criterion, is proportionally as distant from the unit as the variation has been irregular.

The comparison between the group of adjusted subjects (A.G.) and group of maladjusted (M.G.) yielded the following findings:

1. The mean values of d' index on the PM 38 are 1.80 for A.G., and 1.02 for M.G. The difference is statistically significant ($t = 5.02$; $p < .01$). Thus, hypothesis (a) is confirmed.
2. The comparison between means values of beta index on the AEFT (.88 for A.G. and .95 for M.G.; the difference is not significant) and between mean values of beta index on the PM 38 (.98 for A.G. and .92 for M.G.; the difference is not significant) confirm hypothesis (b).
3. The comparison between means values of C index on the AEFT (1.04 for A.G. and 1.03 for M.G.; the difference is not significant) and between mean values of C index on the PM 38 (1.04 for A.G., and 1.15 for M.G.; the difference is not significant), as well, confirm hypothesis (b).
4. The comparison between means values on the EFT (768" for A.G., and 1270" for M.G.; $t = 6.80$; $p < .01$) and d'index on the AEFT (.61 for A.G., and .32 for M.G.; $t = 2.52$; $p < .02$) confirm hypothesis (c).

A second phase of research concerned the study of the learning response in a sample of grammar school students to differentiated didactics, to induce different strategies of processing of the material presented. In particular, didactic units of history were structured according to two models. The first model, a restricted traditional criterion, implied the adoption of an automated learning strategy. The second model, with enlarged criterion, consisted of the presentation of documentary material and material from historical sources, and required the construction of historical information on the part of the pupil. This model implies the adoption of an exploratory strategy for optimal learning. The sample consisted of three experimental classes, with a total of 47 pupils.

A particular methodology for indicating the information processed by the children on the learning trials that followed each didactic unit (3 traditional units and 3 experimental units) allowed us to discern subjects who showed an improvement in learning with the second didactic model, differentiating them from those who remained stable in learning. The modified Raven's Progressive Matrices 38 test was administered to the same subjects to determine their intellective level (d'index) and decision-making strategy (beta index). The test was given immediately following the experimental didactic unit; the subjects were asked to resolve the task using the same modality as that used in the learning test. The EFT was then administered to measure cognitive style.

The experimental hypotheses are as follows: (a) The subjects who improve do not differ in I.Q. from companions who do not improve; (b) the subjects who improve are more field dependent than the subjects who do not improve. In fact, it is on the basis of their more accentuated field dependence that these subjects are able to discern the institutional norm induced with the structural change of the didactic unit; (c) the subjects who improve, adopt an exploratory-type strategy in the learning trial for the experimental didactic unit, whereas their companions who do not improve adopt an automated-type strategy.

The results were:

1. The mean values of d' index on the modified PM 38 are 2.79 for subjects who improve and 2.55 for subjects who do not improve. The difference is not significant. The data confirm hypothesis (a).
2. The mean values on the EFT are 836″ for subjects who improve and 1642″ for subjects who do not improve. The difference is significant ($t = 7.22; p < .01$). The data confirm hypothesis (b).
3. The mean values of beta index on the modified PM 38 are 3.03 for subjects who improve and 13.06 for subjects who do not improve. The difference is significant ($t = 7.95; p < .01$). The data confirm hypothesis c.

On the basis of these results it is possible to redefine the bipolar aspect of cognitive style (differentiation-undifferentiation) with regard to teacher-pupil relationships within the school structure and, more generally, with the dynamics of social systems.

We assume that teachers, as mediators of culture, transmit institutional norms and categorizing information suitable for pursuing organizational objectives at the same time. Now, more differentiated and relatively more field-independent pupils accept categorized information, distinguishing it from institutional norms, thus more adequately accomplishing transformative tasks; less differentiated pupils accept institutional norms and do not distinguish them from categorized information, thus guaranteeing the repetition of the instituted relational modalities. In other terms, more differentiated subjects, as less dependent on the norm and more capable of cognitive restructuring as a function of greater separation between self and non-self, succeed in more effectively using decision-making criteria founded on categorizations according to the principle of noncontradiction (A = presence of signal; Non A = absence of signal and noise). The less differentiated subjects, more dependent on the norm, utilize a criterion founded on affective belonging, the more rigid, the more difficult the effective use of the categories becomes.

CONCLUSION

At this point the relations between bipolar aspects of cognitive style and the articulation of cultural dynamics can be shown. With regard to the latter, a modality is distinguished based on the norm (institutional), i.e., on the value rules according to which an action may be right or wrong (A_x/A_y) and a modality founded on the use of categories (organization), that is, on rules that obey the bivalent logic based on the principle of noncontradiction (A/Non A).

This distinction goes back to the typology of social interactions proposed by Harré and Secord (1972), above all to *ceremonies* and *games*. The first is characterized by structures of actions whose success does not involve an outcome, but is subordinated exclusively to the consensus ("the actions constitute the act only as a result of the social significance attributed to them", p. 49); the second is characterized by actions whose success is subordinated to the presence of a correct and winning, or wrong and losing, outcome.

According to our hypothesis, these different modalities of social interaction are supported by various modes of thought functioning and therefore, of culture, which can be referred to the differentiation-undifferentiation bipolarity. If it is assumed that culture is a system of socially-formulated symbols and referred to objects or states of the internal and external world, an epistemological-type discarding may be singled out relative to the non-isomorphic relationship between symbols and states of the world. This would make it impossible to think of a system of signs or of a social structure, even if highly differentiated, which in itself is effective for the aim of adjustment. From our point of view, it can be affirmed that organismic and cultural structures, according to the differentiation-undifferentiation bipolarity, are characterized by different and complementary advantages for the purpose of adjustment. If the more differentiated structuralizations, due to functional specialization and automation of processes, are more economical in pursuing the planned transformative objectives, the less differentiated structuralizations allow for a more flexible adjustment of the cultural categories and of the decision-making criteria to changes in internal and external states of the world. In other terms, the more or less differentiated subjects with their relations in the social structure, other than resolving differently their adjustment problems, seem to guarantee, in a different and complementary way, the adjustment of social systems to other systems and super-systems with which they interact.

REFERENCES

Abraham, N. (1978). *L'ecorce et le noyau.* Paris: Aubier-Flammarion.

Beretta, A. (1974). La situazione pedagogica dal punto di vista psico-fisiologico, etologico e antropologico. In A. Beretta and M. S. Barbieri (Eds.), *Il centauro e l'eroe.* Bologna: Il Mulino.

Carli, R. (1976). Trasformazione e cambiamento. *Archivio di Psicologia, Neurologia e Psichiatria, 37,* 148–194.

Carli, R., Pizzamiglio, L., & Scolari, G. (1974). Decision strategy and cognitive style. *Giornale Italiano di Psicologia, 2,* 185–193.

Freud, S. (1937) Analisi terminabile e interminabile. In *Opere,* (1979). Vol. XI, p. 495–535. Torino: Boringhieri.

Goodenough, D. R., & Witkin, H. A. (1977). *Origins of the field-dependent and field-independent cognitive styles.* Princeton, NJ: Educational Testing Service (ETS RB 77-9).

Harré, R. & Secord, P. F. (1972). *La spiegazione del comportamento sociale.* Bologna: Il Mulino.

Hochaus, L. (1977). A table for the calculation of d' and beta. *Psychological Bulletin, 77,* 5, 375–376.

Kaës, R. (1973). Quatre études sur la fantasmatique de la formation et le désir de former. In R. Kaës, D. Anzieu, L. V. Thomas, N. Le Guerinel, & J. Filloux (Eds.), *Fantasme et formation.* Paris: Dunod.

Klein, M. (1948). *Contributions to psycho-analysis 1921–1945,* London: Hogarth.

Lo Cascio, G., Carli, R., Arcuri, A., Moggi, D., Randazzo, D., Rovelli, R., Traumuto, R. (1979). *Modelli di valutazione scolastica.* Palermo: Vittorietti.

Mattè Blanco, I. (1975). *The unconscious as infinite sets.* London: Duckworth.

Pelto, P. J. (1968, April). The difference between "tight" and "loose" societies. *Transaction,* 37–40.

Segal, H. (1957). Note on the symbol formation. *International Journal of Psychoanalysis, 38,* 391–397.

Segal, H. (1968). *Introduzione all'opera di Malanie Klein.* Firenze: Martinelli.

Witkin, H. A., Dyk, R. B., Faterson, H. F., Goodenough, D. R., & Karp, S. A. (1962). *Psychological differentiation: Studies of Development.* New York: Wiley.
Witkin, H. A., & Goodenough, D. R. (1977). *Field dependence revisited.* Princeton, NJ: Educational Testing Service (ETS RB 77-16).
Witkin, H. A., Goodenough, D. R., & Oltman, P. K. (1979). Psychological differentiation: Current status. *Journal of Personality and Social Psychology, 37,* 1127-1145.

8 Psychological Differentiation Theory in Social and Cross-Cultural Psychology

Philip K. Oltman
Educational Testing Service, Princeton, New Jersey

The theory of psychological differentiation has generated a large number of studies exploring the implications of the theory for interpersonal behavior. In particular, the field dependence-independence dimension, that aspect of differentiation which expresses the degree of self-nonself segregation, has direct extensions into the interpersonal sphere (Witkin & Goodenough, 1977). Field-independent individuals experience themselves as separate and distinct from others, and they tend to rely on internal referents in interpreting the world around them. Differentiation theory leads us to expect that this cognitive makeup will lead to autonomy in their interpersonal relationships. Field-dependent individuals, on the other hand, have a less separate self and greater reliance on external referents, which we expect will lead to turning toward others for information and guidance in interpreting events. Just as in the perceptual tests of field dependence-independence, where field-dependent people rely more on external frames of reference in making perceptual judgments, so in their interpersonal behavior they rely more on the information provided by others in their social surroundings (Witkin, Goodenough, & Oltman, 1979).

The key concept is an information-processing one, as in the perceptual studies. We ask, what sources of information does the person characteristically rely on to interpret the world? Specific stimuli are understood in the context of some additional information that is brought to bear on them. To the extent that external frames of reference are relied on, this may be observable in the individual's responses. If relatively greater weight is given to internal referents, this too may be evident.

Throughout this chapter, it should be kept in mind that the terms "field dependent" and "field independent" are used for convenience, as labels for the ends of what is really a continuum, and not a dichotomy. It has been said that there are two kinds of people: those who think there are two kinds of people and those who don't. My use of the terms naming the extremes of the distribution is for ease of discussion only, and is not meant to imply a typology.

FIELD DEPENDENCE AND INTERPERSONAL BEHAVIOR

Most of the effects of the link between field dependence-independence and interpersonal behavior can be understood as manifesting the *differing styles of information-seeking* in field-dependent and field-independent people. When information-seeking is not an issue, or when the information that is available is unambiguous, no differences between field-dependent and field-independent people emerge. Thus, there tend to be no differences in dependency as it is usually defined, in response to external reinforcement, in approval-seeking, or in emotional attachment.

What is the case is that, in general, when they need information, field-dependent people look to other people, just as they look to the external field in perceptual tasks. Field-independent people look within themselves, just as they do in perceptual tasks. We can detect these differences in use of information by assessing the type of outcome response or by monitoring the information-gathering attempts made by the individual.

Responsiveness to information from others.   One early example of research in this area employed the autokinetic phenomenon. In this situation, the observer views a point of light in an otherwise dark room. The point seems to wander, but the extent of the observed movement is ambiguous and difficult to quantify because it is subjective. In this study, a confederate gave prearranged judgments of the movement of the light, followed by judgments by the subjects. It was found that field-dependent observers tended to rely more on the judgments of the confederate in making their own responses than did field-independent observers. The external referents provided by the bogus responses of the confederate were there for all to use; however, the field-dependent subjects used them more than did field-independent subjects.

Interestingly, extent of attitude change in response to authoritative sources, bogus group averages, or questionnaire conformity scales have little if any relation to field dependence. Apparently, people must actually interact in order for field dependence to have predictive value; the necessary ingredients are apparently not there in paper-and-pencil situations.

In another example of the effects of differences in responsiveness to other people, subjects were paired in our laboratory to form three kinds of dyads: both members field independent, both members field dependent, or one field independent with one field dependent (Oltman, Goodenough, Witkin, Freedman, & Friedman, 1975). In face-to-face dialogues, they discussed issues about which they initially disagreed, and they were asked to resolve their disagreements during their discussions. The results indicated that the presence of field-independent members in the dyads reduced the frequency of conflict resolutions. That is, dyads reached the most agreements when both partners were field dependent, an intermediate number when one partner was field dependent and one field independent, and the least agreement when both partners were field independent. These latter pairs tended to dislike each other after the discussions, as might be imagined. Field-dependent participants were more likely to accommodate to their partners' views, thereby resolving the conflict and increasing positive feelings.

Here again I should emphasize that field dependent individuals do not simply "go along" under any and all circumstances. Studies have shown that they are not any more cooperative in general, not more hypnotizable, and not stronger placebo reactors. Rather, when they need information, they seek it from others and respond accordingly. When information from outside is not needed to interpret the situation, they do not differ in their behavior from field-independent people.

To highlight the importance of ambiguity, I cite a study (Gates, 1971) in which the participants were asked to talk about a subject that interested them. No other instructions were given to clarify this rather strange request. Field-independent participants produced the same amount of verbal output whether the interviewer was responsive or sat silent. However, field dependents showed much reduced verbal output with the silent interviewer; with no information from the outside, they lacked any confirmation that what they were saying was appropriate. There are other studies with similar results, including indications that field-dependent people, more than field independents, are made anxious by a lack of information from others in ambiguous situations.

Monitoring responses.   One way to find out what people are responding to is to note where they are looking. During difficult problem solving, or in a situation in which the experimenter's behavior provided useful information, field-dependent participants tended to look more at the experimenter than did field independents. It has also been found that field-dependent people prefer to be physically closer to those with whom they are interacting. The field independent among us have probably all had the experience at a cocktail party of being slowly backed into a corner by otherwise charming persons who had a preferred interpersonal distance just a little too close for comfort (assuming of course that we're not so field independent that we never go to cocktail parties at all).

Bias toward social material.   Another indicator of the type of information being monitored is the category of that information, that is, social versus nonsocial. Field-dependent people show better incidental recall for the faces of others with whom they have interacted. This may be a result of their greater attentiveness to other people. They also tend to recall social aspects of situations more than the nonsocial aspects. For example, in incidental learning, field dependents recall more social then neutral words; after an experiment, field dependents recall more social aspects of the situation, while field independents recall task-related aspects; and, when listening to a speaker deliver a speech, field dependents are more influenced by the speaker's performance than by the quality of the argument, while the reverse is true for field independents.

Personal qualities.   What impression do field-dependent and field-independent people give in face-to-face contact? Judges tend to rate field-dependent individuals as sociable, gregarious, and interested in people, while field independents are rated as individualistic, cold, distant, intellectual, and task oriented. Field dependents are more likely to be self-disclosing, to know more people and be known by more, and to prefer team over individual sports. The personal qualities shown by field-dependent people suggest that they would be likable, and this seems to be so.

To summarize in very general terms, we can see from the voluminous literature available that cognitive style is indeed reflected in what people are like as social beings, in ways to be expected from the theory of psychological differentiation. The toward-people orientation of field-dependent individuals is consistent with their generally greater reliance on external referents in interpreting the world around them. The interpersonal autonomy shown by field independents is consistent with their stylistic tendency to rely more on internal referents.

THE CROSS-CULTURAL LITERATURE

We have thus described the interpersonal styles characterizing each end of the dimension, and we turn to studies aimed at the question of how these differences come about (Witkin & Berry, 1975). One approach to this question is through the study of child rearing practices within a culture. Another related approach is to study cultures that differ in their modal cognitive style and look to their child rearing practices for differences that would be expected.

The early studies of child rearing that Hy and his coworkers carried out led to the conclusion that, when there is encouragement within the family for the child to develop separate, autonomous functioning, the child will become relatively field independent. When there is strong emphasis on obedience to parental authority and external control of impulses, the child will likely become relatively field dependent. The key concept from differentiation theory is segregation of self from nonself. The more a family or a culture emphasizes this segregation, the more field independent will its members become.

The field dependence-independence dimension is particularly well suited to cross-cultural investigation for several reasons. It is manifested in a perceptual function that seems to be common among all cultures; it can be assessed by objective procedures; the influence of verbal factors is small; the assessments can be made culture-appropriate; and, relatively similar tasks can be used in many cultures to facilitate comparisons.

The cross-cultural literature can be divided into three rough groupings: studies of ecological factors, studies of societal and cultural factors, and direct studies of child rearing practices in different cultures. These of course are not independent sets of variables, ecological factors influence social organization, which in turn affects the modal style of child rearing.

Ecological factors. The studies of ecological factors are mainly concerned with differences in modal cognitive style between stationary agricultural societies and mobile hunting and gathering groups. The groups studied have usually been subsistence-level societies, which are homogeneous and in which the ecology can be expected to show its influence most clearly.

We can consider these two contrasting ecologies and infer the kinds of cultural organization and personal qualities that would be most adaptive to each. In an environment that is relatively homogeneous, such as the snowfields of the Eskimo or the uniform desert terrain of the Arunta in Australia, an adaptive advantage is conferred on those who have high spatial orientation ability, high personal autonomy, and highly developed restructuring skills. These hunting-gathering groups live in small bands and range widely for food. A complex social hierarchy would be excess baggage under these conditions, and, in fact, these groups emphasize self-reliance and have a rather loose social organization.

In contrast, in a stationary agricultural community, tight control over accumulated food reserves and regulation of interpersonal behavior are important to survival in their close group living conditions. Comparison of the modal cognitive styles of stationary and migratory groups reveals the expected difference, with migratory groups being relatively field independent.

Social and cultural factors. In a related group of studies, the emphasis was on the degree of social conformity which was required of members of the societies. Cultural groups can be arranged along a continuum from "tight" to "loose," reflecting the degree to which social conformity is emphasized. In tight societies, religious authority and political power exert strong control over individual behavior, and obedience is demanded. There are many social roles, and these tend to be hierarchically organized.

In loose societies, role diversity is minimized, with only the barest essentials of social organization being present. Differentiation theory would lead us to expect that the modal cognitive style in tight societies will tend toward field dependence, while that in loose societies will be relatively field independent. It seems likely that societal tightness or looseness exerts its effect on the individual primarily through child rearing practices, and we can now turn to studies focusing on this issue.

Child-rearing.   Again, greater or less pressure toward social conformity is the central issue in these studies. Strictness and strong maternal control of the child's life characterizes the child rearing practices of societies with a relatively field dependent modal cognitive style. Mothers are controlling, intolerant of the child's selection of its own playmates and activities, they value strict obedience, and they do not generally value independence, curiosity, or initiative.

Child rearing in field independent societies is less strict, with little use of physical punishment, and higher valuation of independence on the part of the child. Both mother and father participate directly in the care and training of children. Thus, the child rearing practices of tight and loose societies tend to reflect the organization of the society as a whole. These social and cultural forces leave their imprint on the cognitive makeup of the individual, in ways that can be understood in terms of the theory of psychological differentiation.

Adaptation.   The cross-cultural literature suggests that the modal cognitive style found in a society tends to be suited to the ecology in which that society exists. That is, the culture evolves to suit its ecology, and the individual develops a cognitive makeup to suit the culture. Societies in which people live close together in a fixed location emphasize interpersonal adaptation. Too much independent action would in fact be disruptive under these conditions; the group functions most smoothly when individual behavior is controlled by clear rules that all must follow. On the other hand, migratory groups cannot be encumbered by rigid social hierarchies and prescribed modes of behavior. Their ecology demands self-reliance and an ability to act independently, with an array of spatial skills to guide them in their wanderings. These observations bring us to a point that Hy made repeatedly, especially in recent years. That is, that the field dependence independence cognitive style is value neutral. At each pole of the dimension are to be found qualities which are adaptive under particular dimensions.

CONCLUSION

The progress of Hy's work, from its beginnings in perception, through cognition, personality, social psychology, and cross-cultural psychology, has been a series of ever-widening circles encompassing more diverse phenomena. New data and new ideas led him to enlarge and enrich his theoretical structure to incorporate these developments. His work, and the work of many who were inspired by him, has resulted in a system that has implications for virtually every subfield of psychology.

The basic postulates of his theory of psychological differentiation are quite abstract, dealing as they do with the formal properties of psychological systems. Hy's ability to incorporate such a diverse array of phenomena into his theoretical network bespeaks an impressive degree of restructuring ability, which is found in people with a field-independent cognitive style. But Hy was an exception to his own theory: coexisting with his field-independent cognitive style was a personal warmth and interest in others that touched all of us who were fortunate to have worked with him.

REFERENCES

Gates, D. W. (1971). Verbal conditioning, transfer and operant level "speech style" as functions of cognitive style (Doctoral dissertation, City University of New York, 1971). *Dissertation Abstracts International, 32,* 3634B. (University Microfilms N. 71-30, 719.

Oltman, P. K., Goodenough, D. R., Witkin, H. A., Freedman, N., & Friedman, F. (1975). Psychological differentiation as a factor in conflict resolution. *Journal of Personality and Social Psychology, 32,* 730-736.

Witkin, H. A., & Berry, J. W. (1975). Psychological differentiation in cross-cultural perspective. *Journal of Cross-Cultural Psychology, 6,* 4-87.

Witkin, H. A., & Goodenough, D. R. (1977). Field dependence and interpersonal behavior. *Psychological Bulletin, 84,* 661-689.

Witkin, H. A., Goodenough, D. R., & Oltman, P. K. (1979). Psychological differentiation: current status. *Journal of Personality and Social Psychology, 37,* 1127-1145.

9 Some Implications of Field Dependence for Education

Mario Bertini
University of Rome

The implications of a cognitive style approach to the field of education are broad and specifically articulated. Through the field dependency approach, a number of studies have provided new insights into such relevant aspects as how students learn social material, the use of mediators in learning, the effects of reinforcement, cue salience, how teachers teach, how teachers and students interact, career differentation, educational-vocational interests, educational-vocational choices and achievement, and so on.

A vast body of research bearing on these issues has been reported in the literature, and extensively reviewed by Witkin, Moore, Goodenough and Cox (1977). I do refer to this general review. However, in this chapter my main concentration is on presenting some data on a limited but relevant aspect, viz., that of the process of interaction between teacher and student.

COGNITIVE STYLE AND THE PROBLEM OF TEACHER-STUDENT INTERACTION

The complexity and, quite often, the inadequacy of theoretical and methodological approaches to the problem of "teaching effectiveness" has been repeatedly stated. This complexity has the probability of increasing if one moves from a reactive or mechanistic toward an active or organismic model of man. (Pepper, 1942).

Within a strictly mechanistic stimulus-response mode, where the learner is essentially seen from the beginning as an empty organism ready to respond to appropriate stimuli, teaching effectiveness can be basically assessed as a collection of abilities (generally considered along a continuum of more or less "effective") in the transmission of information. In a sense, it is as if the teacher had these abilities under his skin, independent of the peculiarities under the skin of the learner.

In the organismic model, where, on the contrary, "the individual is viewed as the source of acts, rather than as the collection of acts initiated by external forces" (Reese & Overton, 1970, p. 133), as an agent who treats the information according to individually organized plans, teaching effectiveness must inevitably face the requirements of interaction. In recent years, it has been realized ". . . that many functions traditionally treated as though they belonged to individuals and could thus be studied purely as intrapersonal events, generally occur within an interpersonal context and that it is from this context that they derive their functional meaning" (Schaffer, 1977, p. 3). Therefore, mutuality of differently organized, cognitive and personality systems becomes an important dimension in the analysis of teaching effectiveness.

Certainly, people in education are well aware that teaching effectiveness is a result of a complex interaction among teacher, student and subject to be taught. However, beyond such certain general statements, what we actually need is concrete experimental knowledge of the specific structural factors that play a role in the dynamics of interaction, factors that are often beyond the awareness of the members of that relationship. It is my opinion that a cognitive style approach has something to offer in this direction.

Appropriately rooted in the framework of the organismic model, a cognitive style approach can give us information about the unique ways in which cognition is organized in different individuals. Furthermore, it can give us precious information on how these different organizations influence interaction among individuals. In a sense, a cognitive style approach brings an individual differences perspective to the experimental study of social interaction.

In ordinary usage, style carries the implication that the behavior we are witnessing is an integral part of a broader psychological domain. Thus, styles are ways of characterizing people in a holistic fashion rather than in terms of psychological bits and pieces. As Witkin (1973) stated:

> In the earliest view, when observations of these styles were limited to the cognitive domain, cognitive styles were conceived as the self-consistent modes of functioning an individual shows throughout his perceptual and intellectual activities. Today, we know that cognitive styles are, in fact, manifestations, in the cognitive domain, of still broader dimensions of functioning, which cut across other psychological domains, including personality and social behavior. (p. 2)

So, more than simply cognitive, "they are truly broad personal styles. They are our typical ways of processing information, regardless of whether the information has its primary source in the world outside or within us; and, when in the world outside, regardless of whether the information is provided primarily by things or by persons and their activities" (Witkin, 1973, p. 5).

We have thus far identified a number of cognitive styles. For example: *reflectiveness versus impulsiveness* (Kagan, Rosman, Day, Albert, & Phillips, 1964), the tendency to react to situations slowly, after examining several alternative responses, or rapidly with the first response that comes to mind; *cognitive complexity versus simplicity* (Bieri, 1961), the tendency to view the world along many, or few parameters; *tolerance for unrealistic experiences* (Klein, Gardner, & Schlesinger, 1962), degree of comfort with experiences that are out of the ordinary; *leveling and sharpening* (Gardner, Holzman, Klein, Linton, & Spence, 1959); *serialist-holist* (Pask, 1975); and, finally, Witkin's *field dependence-independence* dimension, which is, by and large, the most extensively investigated cognitive style. In fact, there are around three thousand references in the literature.

FIELD DEPENDENCY AND TEACHER-STUDENT PROCESSES OF INTERACTION

The implications of Witkin's cognitive style approach to the field of education in general and to the more specific area of teacher-student interaction are both broad and specific. The first observation that clearly emerges from the Witkin et al. (1977) review is that cognitive style, without determining degree of sheer teaching competence for the subject to be taught, certainly influences the why or the how teachers with different cognitive styles tend to teach. Some of the different ways in which cognitive styles may affect teaching behavior can be derived from the social versus impersonal orientation and sense of separate identity aspects of the field dependence-independence dimension.

Evidence from studies of teachers' preferences and behavior in simulated teaching situations indicates, first of all, that whereas relatively field-dependent teachers favor teaching situations that allow for interaction with the students, more field-independent teachers prefer teaching situations that are impersonal in nature and oriented toward the more cognitive aspects of teaching. Class discussion, for instance, has been judged by more field-dependent teachers to represent better teaching and to be more effective for learning. A discussion approach, it should be noted, not only emphasizes social interaction, but also gives the students more of a role in structuring the classroom situation. Wu (1968), for example, found that more field-dependent student teachers in social studies ranked discussion as more important to the practice of good teaching than either lecture or discovery approaches, which were favored by more field-independent teachers. Both lecture and discovery approaches reserve much of the organization of the learning situation for the teacher, either through facilitating and guiding student learning or providing information.

In the literature on cognitive styles, other areas have been considered in relation to teaching approaches, such as differences in using correction feedback and/or negative evaluation, etc. On the whole, the evidence gathered suggests that field-dependent and field-independent teachers have different teaching preferences syntonic with their own personal styles, and that, based on these differences, they may conduct their classes differently thereby showing different patterns of actual teaching behavior in the classroom.

On the other side, it is well documented that relatively field-dependent and field-independent students tend to favor different learning approaches in such important areas as use of mediators in learning, learning of social material, cue salience, effects of social reinforcement. The approach favored by one person does not necessarily make for better achievement than the approach favored by another. However, of great relevance for the problem of teaching effectiveness is the consideration of the reciprocal fitness of different preferred learning and teaching strategies.

Learning behavior and teaching behavior are too often studied separately. "For the classroom where teachers and learning are engaged in a continuous, interactive dialogue which constitutes the integral teaching-learning process studies of the combinatory effects of the cognitive styles of both contributors to this process, are likely to be even more informative" (Witkin et al., 1977, p. 32).

Studies of the combinatory effects of cognitive styles have focused mainly on the progress and outcome of an interaction when its participants are matched or mismatched for cognitive style. There is now consistent evidence in the literature that congruency or lack of congruency in cognitive style has a significant influence in various social interaction contexts, such as patient-therapist interactions (Folman, 1973; Greene, 1972), peer interaction, and, in general, in social interaction where participants are working together toward a common goal. Shared interests, shared personality characteristics, and similarity in modes of communication may possibly be the basis for greater interpersonal attraction between individuals of similar cognitive style. Though specific research in the teaching situation is scanty, the evidence accumulated is quite impressive.

DiStefano (1970) used teachers and students as subjects in a regular classroom situation. He found that when they have similar cognitive styles (based on responses to several questionnaires), teachers and students tend to describe each other in positive terms; when they have different cognitive styles, there is a strong tendency to describe each other in negative terms. It is interesting that this applied not only to personal but to intellectual characteristics as well. Teachers often believe that students whose cognitive styles match theirs are smarter than those whose styles are different from theirs. They say that the former are more intelligent, more logical, and more successful as students.

Confirming DiStefano's (1970) finding, James (1973), using a specially-created minicourse in which each teacher taught a class of three field-dependent and three field-independent students, reported that the most field-independent teacher gave all three of his field-independent students higher grades than the three field-dependent students. Conversely, the most field-dependent teacher assigned the three highest grades to his three field-dependent students.

More recently, Packer and Bain (1978) obtained matching effects on objective test performance and on teachers' and students' subjective ratings of each other. Of particular interest in this study is the observation that field-dependent children, who generally do not do well in mathematics, learned mathematics better from a field-dependent than from a field-independent teacher. The fact that mathematics is usually taught by field-independent persons may explain, at least in part, why some students (probably field dependent) show an irrational resistance to enter into the field. Is this resistance due to the lack of congruency in mode of communication between field-independent teachers and field-dependent students?

At any rate, cognitive style matching-mismatching investigations carry interesting implications for how comfortably a student may deal with a particular teacher, how influenced the teacher may be in the assessment process, how a student may learn better with a particular teacher. Therefore, I think they also raise relevant questions regarding teaching effectiveness. Perhaps we should not think in terms of good teachers and bad teachers, or good students and bad students, but rather good or bad teachers for which kind of students, and good or bad students for which kind of teacher.

Research Findings

To this area of reciprocal interaction a further complexity is added if we consider the sex factor in combination with cognitive style. This is precisely what I and my collaborators attempted to do in a recent study. Some preliminary findings follow.

In line with DiStefano's (1970) work, we used descriptive questionnaires to obtain information about reciprocal students' and teachers' attraction components. Like James (1973), we considered the teacher's assessment of the students' actual performance as reported by grading. However, as a departure from both of these studies, (a) we studied the influence of the sex variable both of teachers and of students in interaction with their respective cognitive styles, and (b) we used a much larger sample.

Consider a brief outline of our methodology and results. We tested 438 students at the secondary school level and 98 teachers on an extensive battery of cognitive style measures. We then had teachers and students complete three descriptive questionnaires. A factor analysis, performed separately for teachers and students, resulted in the development of some scales on which a four-factor analysis of variance was carried out (student sex, teacher sex, student cognitive style, teacher cognitive style). Based on the preliminary findings, a powerful interaction effect between sex and cognitive style factors is apparently involved, both in the teachers' assessments of the students and in the students' assessments of the teachers.

Teachers' Assessment of Students

The influence of the aforementioned factors is apparent at the teacher level, at the student level, and at the teacher by student interaction level. In the following presentation of findings, the teacher assessments exemplified are mental efficiency, sociability, positive evaluation, liking, final grades and negative evaluation. Only one scale — liking — is illustrated for student ratings of teachers.

Teacher level. If we consider the teachers' assessment scores independent of the specific characteristics of the assessed students, some significant differences emerge in relation to their cognitive style and/or sex. For instance, Table 9.1 shows the statistically significant influence of the interplay between teacher's sex and teacher's cognitive style in determining the mean level of scores utilized by the teachers in assessing the students' mental efficiency. The scale contains such terms as rational, successful, active, logical, etc. The table shows a significant interaction between teacher's sex and cognitive style ($p < .01$). There is a trend for field-independent female teachers to use high scores on this scale, as compared not only with field-dependent females but also field-dependent and field-independent males.

TABLE 9.1
Relation between Teachers' Sex and Cognitive
Style on Their Description of Students'
Mental Efficiency

		Teachers	
		F.D.	*F.I.*
Teachers	Males	760	765
	Females	687	784

It is interesting to note that on the sociability scale (Table 9.2), on the contrary, field-dependent male teachers tend to give highest scores to the students. The interaction between teacher's sex and teacher's cognitive style is significant ($p < .01$). A tendency for the teachers to overevaluate — in a sense to project onto the students — the characteristics of their own personality not congruent with culturally-mediated sex-role assignments might be an interesting interpretation of these findings.

Student level. Teachers' perception of the students seems significantly influenced in a predictable way by the interaction between cognitive style and sex of the same students. So, for instance, on the positive evaluation scale, (Table 9.3), a field-independent boy is more highly evaluated by the teacher than a field-independent girl, whereas a field-dependent boy is much less positively evaluated than a field-dependent girl. The interaction between student's sex and student's cognitive style is significant at $p < .05$.

A similar tendency can be seen for the "liking" scale, (Table 9.4). The interaction between student's sex and student's cognitive style is significant at $p < .05$. Boys and girls are approximately equally liked if they are field independent, but a strong difference can be observed if they are field dependent.

TABLE 9.2
Relation of Teachers' Sex and Cognitive
Style on Their Description of Students'
on a "Sociability" Scale

		Teachers	
		F.D.	F.I.
	Males	172	147
Teachers			
	Females	151	159

TABLE 9.3
Relation of Students' Sex and Cognitive Style to
Teachers' Description of Student on a
"Positive" Evaluation Scale

		Students	
		Boys	Girls
	F.D.	2609	2756
Students			
	F.I.	2906	2876

TABLE 9.4
Relation between Students' Sex and Cognitive
Style to Teachers' Description of Students on a
"Liking" Scale

		Students	
		Boys	Girls
Students	F.D.	686	741
	F.I.	773	775

A field-dependent girl is liked much more by the teacher than a field-dependent boy, who is actually the least accepted in the pattern.

On the mental efficiency scale, (Table 9.5), the interaction between student's sex and student's cognitive style is significant ($p < .01$). A field-independent boy is perceived as more mentally efficient than a field-independent girl, whereas a field-dependent girl is perceived as much more mentally efficient than a field-dependent boy.

And finally, the striking influence of sex as a mediating factor is apparent also in the final grading (Table 9.6). The interaction between student's sex

TABLE 9.5
Relation of Students' Sex and Cognitive Style to
Teachers' Description of Students on a
"Mental Efficiency" Scale

		Students	
		Boys	Girls
Students	F.D.	666	732
	F.I.	808	786

TABLE 9.6
Relation between Students' Sex and Cognitive
Style on Teachers' Assessment of
Students' Final Grading

		Students	
		Boys	Girls
Students	F.D.	5.84	6.38
	F.I.	6.79	6.72

and cognitive style is significant at $p < .05$. Field-independent boys receive higher grades than girls, and field-dependent girls receive much higher grades than boys. The penalty suffered by field-independent girls and field-dependent boys, respectively, is obvious. It is worth noting that no main effect for student's sex appeared in any of these descriptions. It is the specific combination of cognitive style and sex that influences the way in which students are perceived by their teachers. It is possible, then, that cultural sex-role stereotypes influence teachers' assessments of students in a significant way, at least in this specific population.

Teachers by students interaction level.   On the negative evaluation scale (Table 9.7), a suggestive pattern of interaction significant at the $< .01$ level emerges between teachers' sex, teachers' cognitive style, students' sex, students' cognitive style. Whereas field-dependent male teachers tend to reject more female students and field-independent male teachers tend to reject more male students, field-dependent female teachers seem to reject more male students and field-independent female teachers seem to reject more female students. Stated differently, according to the table, it seems that, whereas field-dependent teachers tend to reject students of the opposite sex, field-independent teachers tend to reject students of the same sex. According to these data, the teachers' cognitive style seems to play a significant role in determining the way in which students of different sex are perceived.

As we can see in Table 9.8, significant effects ($p < .05$) between teachers' sex, teachers' cognitive style and students' cognitive style are also evident in the final grading. A way of reading this table may be the following: Whereas for the male teachers matching in cognitive style seems to have a slight positive influence in the assessment of students (difference in favor of field-independent students becomes attenuated when the assessing teacher is field-

TABLE 9.7
Relation of Teachers' Sex and Students' Cognitive Style to
Teachers' Description of Students on "Negative Evaluation" Scale

			Students	
			Boys	*Girls*
	Males	F.D.	371	389
		F.I.	394	370
Teachers				
	Females	F.D.	389	369
		F.I.	368	391

Note: The higher the score, the more negative the evaluation.

TABLE 9.8
Relation of Teachers' Sex, Teachers' Cognitive Style and Students'
Cognitive Style to Teachers' Assessment of
Students' Final Grading

			Students	
			F.D.	*F.I.*
	Males	F.D.	6.50	6.95
		F.I.	6.18	6.86
Teachers				
	Females	F.D.	5.13	6.45
		F.I.	7.00	6.77

TABLE 9.9
Relation of Male/Female Students' Descriptions on a "Liking"
Scale of Teachers Who Differ in Sex and Cognitive Style

			Teachers	
			F.D.	*F.I.*
	Boys	Males	444	448
		Females	443	459
Students				
	Girls	Males	424	447
		Females	465	451

dependent), an opposite influence seems to emerge when the teachers are female. Field-dependent females give higher grades to field-independent students, whereas field-independent females give higher grades to field dependent students.

Students' Assessments of Teachers

On the other side of the coin, looking at the students' description of the teachers, we have a striking confirmation of the interaction between student's sex, teacher's sex and teacher's cognitive style ($p < .01$). As an example, in Table 9.9 we can see how boys and girls are differently influenced by the sex-cognitive style interaction with their teachers. Whereas boys seem generally more attracted by the field-independent cognitive style (even more so if this style is carried by female teachers), surprisingly, the girls seem to make a clear distinction; they tend to prefer field dependence in the female teachers and field independence in the male teachers. As can be seen, the girls definitely do not like field-dependent male teachers.

CONCLUSIONS

Evidence can be found in the literature that ". . . characteristics of the teacher — in particular his cognitive style — may influence his proficiency with different types of prescribed instructional approaches, may influence his free choice of instructional approaches, may influence his incidental behavior in a way which interacts directly with characteristics of the students" (Packer & Bain, 1978, p. 865).

On the whole, the evidence gathered should convince us of the importance of taking a teacher's cognitive style into account when considering teaching effectiveness, especially if we follow a modern approach to this area that tends to emphasize interaction rather than to exalt competence in a vacuum. However, once the fact is acknowledged that cognitive style does influence teaching effectiveness, two important questions must be raised: (a) What contribution can a cognitive style approach make to the goal of increasing teaching effectiveness? (b) What eventual contribution can the cognitive style approach make to the assessment of teacher effectiveness?

More specifically, the first question can be phrased as: What should we do with the knowledge of combinatory effects of teachers' and students' cognitive styles? Should we take practical steps in class grouping?

To have demonstrated that a match-mismatch phenomenon exists, as Witkin et al. (1977) say, ". . . is to have opened the door only a crack" (pp. 35–36). What is already visible through that crack suggests, however, that we may find much of interest behind it for the teaching-learning process.

However, there are many basic questions to be answered before we can begin to consider the practical implications of the match-mismatch phenomenon for the classroom situation. The first and foremost question is whether matching for cognitive style makes for better student learning and not only for the greater interpersonal attraction that has been mainly demonstrated. It is certainly possible to see ways in which the teacher-student match may have a positive learning outcome. Among others, The Packer and Bain (1978) findings on the teaching of mathematics are a brilliant demonstration of this. On the other hand, it is equally possible to conceive of negative consequences of matching. Witkin et al. (1977) give some examples of this:

It may be that for some kinds of learning content a contrast in styles between teacher and student may be more stimulating than similarity. In general, because heterogeneity makes for diversity in viewpoints and responses, it may serve to make the classroom more lively; if so, homogeneous classes may be ill-advised. As another example, while the interpersonal effects of the discussion approach used by relatively field-dependent teachers may be helpful to learning by field-dependent students, that approach at the same time minimizes the structure from the teacher which field-dependent students seem to need for most effective learning. As still another example, we have seen that relatively field-independent teachers are likely to use negative reinforcement in the classroom, but it is the more field-dependent student who is particularly responsive to this technique; although dependent on circumstances, its effect on learning may be positive or negative. There is a similar "disparity" in the more field-independent teachers' tendency to provide feedback and the field dependent child's benefit from feedback as a source of structuring. (p. 36)

The general pattern of teacher-student interaction becomes even more complex if we consider some moderating or situational variables that can significantly modify the cognitive style match-mismatch effects. One such variable is course curriculum: "In areas where good student performance requires highly specialized skills, the availability of these skills may overcome cognitive style match-mismatch effects" (Witkin et al., 1977, p. 37).

Another very important variable that is likely to modify and complicate the pattern of interaction is certainly that related to sex of both teachers and students. Our own research seems to provide support for this.

I also believe that the problem of match-mismatch should be enlarged into a more complex and more naturalistic perspective. We should not follow a mechanical point of view as if students' and teachers' cognitive styles were pieces or parts to fit together, but we should see these differences in cognitive styles as more or less mobile starting points for complex transactions.

Leaving the complex questions of "matching" aside for the moment, it is still possible to see the important contribution that a cognitive style approach makes to the understanding and handling of the teacher-student interaction processes. Based on already available knowledge, a variety of strategies could be developed with the aim of increasing the awareness of such processes in the school system protagonists.

The sensitizing of the teacher, and perhaps the student, to the complexity of reciprocal interaction, and equipping them with some specific tools for handling those interactions indeed seems an important step toward achieving the goal of increased teacher effectiveness. It is not unreasonable to expect that as teachers become more aware of the way cognitive style fosters their own teaching approaches, as well as shapes students' learning preferences, they may become more effective in adapting instructional procedures to the needs of these different kinds of students.

The issue of teacher adaptation has not yet been investigated, but some evidence from research on the therapist-patient relationship (Witkin, Lewis, & Weil, 1968) suggests that this line of research may be a fruitful one. In the words of Witkin et al., (1977): "Beyond encouraging teachers to adapt their teaching to students as they find them, we may hope even more that teachers may find ways of helping students diversify their learning strategies" (p. 31). They go on:

> We do not yet know what needs to be done, or how far it is possible to progress in training students to move outside the channels into which we now find them directed by their cognitive styles. The apparent malleability of learning strategies flowing from cognitive styles encourages us to believe that such movement can be achieved. We do not assume that everyone can take equally well to all domains or that it is a desirable goal of education to create a universe of Jacks-of-all-trades. However, for the educator, the development of greater diversity in behaviors within individuals seems as important an objective as the recognition and utilization of diversity among individuals. (p. 53)

On the basis of these premises, a second important contribution relevant to the assessment of teacher effectiveness may be the degree of teacher flexibility in the task of shifting strategies emanating from both cognitive styles. "We may wonder whether these are individual differences among teachers in the ease with which they are able to determine that a shift from the teaching approach fostered by their cognitive styles is required and then to make the shift" (Witkin et al., 1977, p./32).

Within the bipolarity of the field-dependence-independence dimension developed by Witkin and Goodenough (1981), the modern concept of mobility and fixity (that is, the concept that there are people more or less mobile and more or less fixed at the poles of the dimension) may be profitably utilized in this regard.

In conclusion, more and more in modern psychology, linear, sequential, causative models tend to be replaced by circular interactive models that emphasize the relational aspects between subjects and events of which the former are protagonists; for instance, behavior of student B may be seen not only as stimulus of, but also as response to the anticipated behavior of teacher A. If these concepts seem to enter into the schools, what we need is concrete, experimental knowledge of the specific structural factors that play a role in the dynamics of interaction, often going beyond the awareness of the members of the relationship itself.

The modern view clearly fostered by a cognitive style approach may contribute to freeing the teaching relationship from its authoritarian atmosphere, by joining the protagonists of the relationship in a pattern of reciprocal influences within which, though at different levels of responsibility, both teachers and students are significantly involved.

I would like to end this chapter by emphasizing Hy Witkin's words (Witkin et al., 1977): "...the development of greater diversity in behaviors within individuals seems as important an objective as the recognition of diversity among individuals" (p. 53).

And not many teachers did more than Hy to bring to expression the hidden potentialities of people while at the same time respecting their individuality.

REFERENCES

Bieri, J. (1961). Complexity-simplicity as a personality variable in cognitive and preferential behavior. In D. W. Fiske & S. R. Maddi (Eds.), *Functions of varied experience*. Homewood, IL: Dorsey Press.

DiStefano, J. J. (1970). Interpersonal perceptions of field independent and field dependent teachers and students. (Doctoral dissertation, Cornell University, 1969). *Dissertation Abstracts International, 31,* 463-A. (University Microfilms No. 70-11, 225)

Folman, R. Z. (1973). Therapist-patient perceptual style, interpersonal attraction, initial interview behavior, and premature termination. (Doctoral dissertation, Boston University, 1973). *Dissertation Abstracts International, 34,* 1746B. (University Microfilms No. 73-23, 482)

Gardner, R., Holzman, P., Klein, G., Linton, D., & Spence, D. (1959). Cognitive control: A study of individual consistencies in cognitive behavior. *Psychological Issues,* (Monograph 4) New York: International Press.

Greene, M. A. (1972). Client perception of the relationship as a function of worker-client cognitive styles. (Doctoral dissertation, Columbia University, 1972). *Dissertation Abstracts International, 33,* 3030A-3031A. (University Microfilms No. 72-31, 213)

James, C. D. R. (1973). *A cognitive style approach to teacher-pupil interaction and the academic performance of black children.* Unpublished master's thesis, Rutgers University.

Kagan, J., Rosman, B. L., Day, D., Albert, J., & Phillips, W. (1964). Information processing in the child: Significance of analytic and reflective attitudes. *Psychological Monographs, 78,* 1 (Whole No. 56).

Klein, G. C., Gardner, R. W., & Schlesinger, H. J. (1962). Tolerance for unrealistic experiences: A study of the generality of cognitive controls. *British Journal of Psychology, 53,* 41-55.

Packer, J., & Bain, J. (1978). Cognitive style and student-teachers compatibility. *Journal of Educational Psychol., 70* (5), 864-871.

Pask, G. (1975). *Conversation, cognition and learning: Cybernetic theory and methodology.* Amsterdam: Elsevier.

Pepper, S. C. (1942). *World hypotheses.* Berkeley: University of California Press.

Reese, H. W., & Overton, W. F. (1970). Models of development and theories of development. In L. R. Goulet & P. B. Baltes (Eds.), *Life span developmental psychology.* NY: Academic Press.

Schaffer, H. (1977). *Studies in mother-infant interaction.* London: Academic Press.

Witkin, H. A. (1973). *Evaluation and guidance from a cognitive-style perspective.* Unpublished manuscript.

Witkin, H. A., & Goodenough, D. R. (1981). *Cognitive styles: Essence and origins. Field dependence and field independence.* New York: International Universities Press.

Witkin, H. A., Moore, C. A., Goodenough, D. R., Cox, P. W. (1977). Field dependent and field independent cognitive styles and their educational implications. *Review of Educational Research, 47,* 1-64.

Witkin, H. A., Lewis, H. B., & Weil, E. (1968). Affective reactions and patient-therapist interactions among more differentiated and less differentiated patients early in therapy. *Journal of Nervous and Mental Disease, 146* (3), 193-208.

Wu, J. J. (1968). Cognitive style and task performance: A study of student teachers. (Doctoral dissertation, University of Minnesota, 1967). *Dissertation Abstracts, 29,* 176A. (University Microfilms, No. 68-7408)

10 Counseling Implications of Field Dependence-Independence in an Educational Setting

Evelyn Raskin
Brooklyn College City University of New York

The potential practical value of measures of field dependence-independence in educational and career guidance is evident. It is implied in the theoretical formulations about this dimension. It also emerges from the empirical studies that Hy Witkin carried out to validate hypotheses concerning the personal characteristics associated with field dependence and field independence. Although abundant literature has accumulated over the past few years on the role of cognitive style in career differentiation, the focus of my remarks is on the unique longitudinal study with which I am familiar.

In the middle 1960s, when Hy first proposed the possibility of a long-term longitudinal study of academic careers, we, or at least I, thought of such a study as contributing relevant evidence for the "construct validity" of field dependence-independence. Academic fields of concentration that make differential demands on cognitive skills and personality characteristics seemed to offer an ideal opportunity to determine the ways in which field dependence-independence would express itself in real life behavioral situations. But I believe that Hy was already thinking of opening up a new frontier for the psychological implications and applications of cognitive style. In conjunction with the voluminous data available from other studies inspired by Hy's work, the results of our longitudinal study encouraged him and others on our team to believe that a knowledge of an individual's cognitive style can be practically useful to both student and counselor in identifying and selecting appropriate educational and career goals.

In the basic study undertaken in 1967 (Witkin et al., 1977b), we accomplished what initially seemed to me impossible: administering a form of the Group Embedded Figures Test (GEFT) to virtually the entire freshman class of approximately 1,600 students enrolled in a famous but anonymous institution—a large municipal college. But, as all of his colleagues have experienced, Hy had a way of summoning forth energies in us that we did not know we possessed. Data were obtained on the students' preliminary choice of a major as well as their Scholastic Aptitude Test (SAT) scores. Approximately 4 years later, we examined the transcripts of 1,400 students in that entering class of 1967 who had won the glittering prize—graduation. The transcripts provided data on final major choice, grades, and, for 634 of these students, applications for professional or graduate schools. Those who went on to postgraduate work were thus identified, and information on their status and subsequent progress was obtained.

These data enabled us to determine the degree to which cognitive style, as measured by a test of field dependence-independence, predicted three features of students' academic histories: (a) chosen major fields at time of entry, at graduation, and at enrollment in graduate school; (b) stability of the initial choice; and (c) differential academic achievement.

Major fields were classified into three groups according to their apparent similarity in content and our judgment of requirements with respect to the distinguishing characteristics of field dependence-independence. The first two groups consisted of courses of study that stressed primarily cognitive restructuring skills and those which, in contrast, stressed interpersonal relations and skills. Thus, natural sciences and mathematics constituted one group, making demands primarily on restructuring abilities. Education (predominantly elementary education) was a second group, whose content emphasized interpersonal relations in everyday activities and required relatively limited restructuring skills. A third intermediate group, like psychology, was identified that could draw on either field-dependent or field-independent characteristics. Major fields for which no relation to cognitive style seemed obvious or could be expected were also included in this third intermediate, or "other" category.

Our findings, briefly summarized, were as follows:

1. Measures of field dependence-independence by and large did not predict choices of major fields at *college entry* more effectively than did the student's SAT-M or -V scores. When GEFT scores were adjusted for SAT differences, the mean differences between the three groups of major fields at time of college entry were insignificant.

2. But GEFT scores did contribute to predicting choice of major at college graduation and field of specialization in graduate school, even when adjustments for differences in SAT scores were made. Thus, the highest mean GEFT score was obtained by the students who eventually majored or specialized in science and math; the "other" group was next; and education majors both in college and graduate school were most field dependent. Knowledge of a student's level of field dependence-independence at college entry thus can

supplement information provided by aptitude scores in predicting subsequent academic choices, including major fields at the time of college graduation and graduate school.

With respect to stability of student major choice, our data showed that those who chose science initially and stayed with it were more field independent than those who shifted their majors by graduation or who had dropped out of college — even after GEFT scores were again adjusted for differences in scholastic aptitude measures. Similarly, those preliminary science majors who went on to graduate work in science had significantly higher GEFT scores than those who entered other graduate school specialties, again after adjustment for SAT variables. The findings in education seem especially interesting. (Most of the students who chose education in the 1960s were women; our analysis was confined to women students.) Those education majors who did not shift tended to be more field dependent than those who crossed over to other fields such as art or music.

These findings indicate that if entering college students have selected science or education as their preliminary majors, a knowledge of their cognitive style may help a counselor predict whether they will graduate with the same major, and whether, if they do graduate work, they will also continue in that discipline. Our data further suggest that students shift their majors over the course of their college careers in directions more compatible with their cognitive styles. Thus, the most field-independent "shifters" tended to change their majors to music, art, and science, whereas the most field-dependent "shifters" tended to change their majors to education and the humanities. Shifts were more common out of mathematics and science than the other way around. In these disciplines, which require restructuring skills, there is no refuge for field-dependent persons. In the social sciences, however, there is more accommodation for both field-dependent and field-independent people.

One question obviously begging for answers is the nature of the process that eventually draws students towards fields congruent with their cognitive styles. From our data, as well as from many other published reports, we know that GEFT scores are not related to overall academic achievement as measured by the gross 4-year Grade Point Average. Cognitive styles have more value in guidance than in selection, unless we are thinking of selection for specialized academic or vocational settings. However, we might expect GEFT scores to be correlated with achievement in specific courses in which students with different cognitive styles could function best.

After SAT-M scores were partialled out, correlations between grades in introductory mathematics and physics courses and GEFT scores were low but significant. Similarly, the correlations between grades in introductory education courses and GEFT scores were low and insignificant although in the expected negative direction. In any event, unsatisfactory performance, as reflected in grades, did not seem to account substantially for students' leaving initial majors to enter those more compatible with their cognitive styles. This finding may result from the unreliability of grades as a measure of achievement (particularly during the turbulent years of the 1970s) as well as the homogeneity of our samples. Assessment of such factors as realistic self-appraisal of abilities, knowledge of vocational requirements, and experiences in introductory courses through interviews with these students might reveal more of the process by which they eventually gravitate toward fields more congenial to their cognitive style.

Since our longitudinal study began, however, many studies have appeared which report that relatively field-independent students do perform significantly better in the mathematics, science, and engineering fields than do field-dependent students. Unfortunately, there are relatively few studies on performance in educational-vocational areas in which a predominantly social orientation would result in superior performance. One reason for this, as Hy suggested, may be that the fields to which field dependent students are attracted are what he calls broad-gauge disciplines, in which there is a great diversity of subject matter. In psychology, for example, a student can concentrate on either traditional experimental courses or those more clinically oriented.

The literature since our study was undertaken is also replete with findings from cross-sectional studies with student populations different from ours but that confirm the evidence of the longitudinal study. On standard interest inventories such as the Strong Vocational Interest Blank, field-independent students consistently express interest in the mathematical and scientific cluster of occupations, whereas field-dependent students show relatively strong interests in the welfare-helping-humanitarian cluster, as well as in so-called "persuasive" and administrative activities. Relationships between cognitive style and expressed vocational interest measures are highest when the vocational interest measures reflect both the cognitive and social characteristics that combine at each end of the dimension of field dependence-independence.

We carried out a supplementary analysis (Goodenough et al., 1979) of our data on students who at college entry designated the specific vocational choice of pre-medical study. (There were so few pre-med women students that they were not included in the data analysis. Today, from 25 to 50% of an entering pre-medical class may consist of women – a dramatic change in 13 years and one that would have pleased Hy immensely.) Our follow-up study shows that knowledge of an individual's cognitive style can help predict the evolution of an initial vocational goal or choice that is specific. Specific choices are firmer expressions of educational-vocational orientation and commitment than are expressed interests. The male freshmen pre-meds were no different in their cognitive style from those who designated other career choices. However, by the end of their college careers, senior pre-meds were more field independent than other seniors. Medical school applicants were more field independent than nonapplicants, and those who enrolled were similarly more field independent than those who did not. The differences remained even after adjustments in SAT-V and -M scores. When the data were analyzed for the approximately 140 male pre-meds at college entry, only a small percentage of those who were most field dependent finally applied to or enrolled in medical schools (11% and 3%, respectively). Thus, cognitive style measures have a stronger relation with actual entry into a vocation such as medicine than with initial expressed interest. This is consistent with our earlier reported finding that final major choice corresponds more closely to cognitive style than to preliminary choice, which represents primarily an expression of interest.

This work carried out by Hy in collaboration with his associates, as well as the corroborative evidence that his work has stimulated and which I have only partially summarized, leads to the conclusion that cognitive styles can play an independent and significant role in the complex process by which many students evolve and eventually arrive at satisfactory career choices during undergraduate and post-graduate years.

Hy has pointed out (Witkin, 1974) additional advantages that cognitive style measures possess as potentially valuable tools in helping both students and counselors identify suitable educational and career goals. As compared with conventional psychometric measures, tests like the Embedded Figures Test (EFT) are not only objective and quantitative in nature, but they are essentially nonverbal. For this reason, they seem particularly valuable in counseling the verbally disadvantaged students in our educational institutions. (This feature was important to Hy, who was deeply concerned by the penalty inflicted on disadvantaged students by our verbally loaded assessment procedures.) The lack of transparency in cognitive style measures obtained from the EFT also confers on it an advantage that conventional interest test scales do not possess. They are value free, or rather, not value biased. By this, Hy meant that the continuum of scores on the EFT does not go from success to deficiency or failure. Valuable but different adaptive capacities are measured at each end of this dimension. Thus, a student with a relatively low score on the GEFT need not be made anxious or feel threatened; on the contrary, the counselor would interpret this score as signifying the positive assets of interest in people and sensitivity to the social aspects of situations. Better still, Hy would have wanted a standardized test in which a field-dependent approach would be required for successful performance resulting in high scores.

The richness of the available evidence leads me to encourage counselors in educational settings to use tests of field dependence-independence in their battery of diagnostic instruments. But this advice is subject to some caveats.

Although there is substantial evidence that measures of field dependence-independence predict fields of educational and even vocational specialization, there is, nevertheless, limited information on the relationship between cognitive style measures and actual performance in both academic and actual vocational settings. We need, particularly, more information about courses and fields in which field-dependent people actually excel in their performance. Other, related, practical problems need to be pursued in order to increase the value of field dependence-independence measures in counseling. More work needs to be done in determining the psychological characteristics required in different major fields and vocations. And more valid measures of successful performance need to be developed in such fields as the social sciences and management or administration.

Finally, in using measures of cognitive style in educational and vocational guidance, I reiterate the important cautionary note sounded by Hy. He was most sensitive to the dangers of locking people into fields compatible with their cognitive styles. In his most recent papers (Witkin, Goodenough, & Oltman, 1979; Witkin, Moore, Goodenough, & Cox, 1977a), he spoke about the possibility of producing change, flexibility, and mobility in cognitive styles by means of appropriate training procedures. For example, field-dependent people, who are likely to avoid mathematics, perhaps should be taught mathematics by different methods and approaches adapted to their cognitive style and by teachers whose teaching methods and cognitive styles are congenial to field-dependent students. And we all know physicians whose restructuring skills need to be complemented by training in sensitivity to people and in empathy.

If cognitive style is to be used as an adjunct in counseling, it should be applied in ways that express the well-defined and beautifully contoured central themes of Dr. Witkin's work and life: respect for diversity among individuals — in his own words, the recognition that "in carrying out society's manifold tasks there is a place for each of us"; second, and equally important, the application of cognitive style to a counseling approach directed toward enhancing and enlarging the rich spectrum of developmental possibilities *within* each individual.

REFERENCES

Goodenough, D. R., Oltman, P. K., Friedman, F., Moore, C. A., Witkin, H. A., Owen, D., & Raskin, E. (1979). Cognitive styles in the development of medical careers. *Journal of Vocational Behavior, 14,* 341–351.

Witkin, H. A. (1974). A cognitive style perspective on evaluation and guidance. *Proceedings of the 1973 Invitational Conference on Testing Problems — Measurement for Self-understanding and Personal Development.* Princeton, NJ: Educational Testing Service, 21–27.

Witkin, H. A., Goodenough, D. R., & Oltman, P. K. (1979). Psychological differentiation: Current status. *Journal of Personality and Social Psychology, 37,* 1127–1145.

Witkin, H. A., Moore, C. A., Goodenough, D. R., & Cox, P. W. (1977a). Field-dependent and field-independent cognitive styles and their educational implications. *Review of Educational Research, 47,* 1–64.

Witkin, H. A., Moore, C. A., Oltman, P. K., Goodenough, D. R., Friedman, F., Owen, D. R., & Raskin, E. (1977b). Role of the field-dependent and field-independent cognitive styles in academic evolution: A longitudinal study. *Journal of Educational Psychology, 69,* 197–211.

11 Herman Witkin and the Meaning of Style

Samuel Messick
Educational Testing Service, Princeton, New Jersey

This volume has provided an impressive summary of Herman Witkin's impressive contributions to perceptual, social, crosscultural, clinical, and counseling psychology. Hy had the insight to descry that the enormous individual differences evident in the way people determine the upright in space provides a veritable window into the personality. He conceived of these individual differences in orientation to the upright as a dimension of field dependence versus field independence, which he gradually came to understand through three decades of programmatic research: first as a dimension of field versus body orientation in the resolution of perceptual cue conflicts; then as a dimension of analytical restructuring; then as an articulated versus global field approach; and ultimately as a dimension of self-differentiation leading to autonomy from external information sources, whether perceptual or interpersonal. He viewed this dimension as a contrast between dynamic Gestalts, to use Philip Vernon's felicitous phrase, with the field-independent person being analytical, self-referent, and impersonal in orientation and the field-dependent person being global, socially sensitive, and interpersonal in orientation. By thus focusing attention on the manner or mode of cognition rather than on the content or level of cognition, and by noting that the positive and adaptive features associated with each pole of this contrast rendered the variable value neutral, he formally affirmed field dependence versus field independence as a dimension of cognitive style. By systematically refining this dimension of cognitive style, he simultaneously refined the whole concept of cognitive style as a bridge between perception and personality, between cognition and affect, between socialization and social behavior.

In many ways the programmatic research strategy that Hy employed was a field-independent strategy in the sense that it was construct-referent instead of self-referent — other variables were to be understood by virtue of their relation to the central concept of field-dependence-independence and as the network of relationships expanded, restructurings occurred to maintain construct self-consistency.

In order to comprehend the full import of Hy's contribution, we recall the context from which it emerged. Three major traditions provide the historical underpinnings for work on cognitive styles. The first tradition is the psychology of individual differences, as epitomized by the studies of Thurstone and Cattell, both of whom uncovered factorial dimensions similar to field independence. These factor analysts viewed such dimensions in terms of consistent individual differences, which they were, but Witkin in addition saw them as different individual consistencies. He thus viewed field dependence in particular and cognitive styles in general in terms of both individual differences and intraindividual consistencies, with extraordinarily fruitful results.

A second tradition is psychoanalytic ego psychology, wherein cognitive styles were viewed as organizing and regulating variables in ego adaptation to the environment. Witkin resonated to this notion and proceeded to relate the cognitive style of field dependence-independence to consistencies in the expression and control of impulses, to the form of preferred defense mechanisms, and to type of symptom formation, without at the same time limiting himself to strict psychoanalytic formulations.

The third tradition is the experimental psychology of cognition, with an emphasis on regularities in information processing. Within this tradition of cognitive psychology, the Gestalt movement was particularly influential for Hy because of his personal association with both Köhler and Wertheimer. These direct intellectual roots in Gestalt psychology sensitized Hy to issues of form in cognition and led him to view individual consistencies in the manner or form of perceiving and thinking as critical psychological phenomena, a personological leap far beyond the temper of his Gestalt mentors. These ideas contributed to and were nourished by an emergent new movement ascendant at the time, namely the so-called New Look in perception, which underscored the formative role of needs and values in perceiving. The concept of cognitive style added the prospect that the expression of needs and values in perception was itself moderated by stylistic regulatory features of the personality, thereby spotlighting the perceiver in perceptual theory.

Herman Witkin brought distinct, and not always congenial, intellectual traditions into integrated focus, capitalized on the distinctive features of each, and extended their import empirically into new domains through a series of developmental, clinical, and cross-cultural studies.

I once heard a noted perceptual psychologist remark that cognitive styles were exciting concepts, but that too many unfulfilled promissory notes had been issued in their name. This may well be true for some cognitive styles, perhaps even for most of them, but it is not true for field dependence-independence. Its early promise has been fulfilled, and its potential continues to offer ample collateral for exciting new forays. That, we owe to Herman Witkin. That is his intellectual legacy.

12 Epilogue: Relation of Witkin's Work to Future Trends in Psychology

Mario Bertini
Luigi Pizzamiglio
University of Rome

Seymour Wapner
Clark University

The chapters presented in this book speak strongly of Hy Witkin's contributions to psychology. These voices are echoed in the vast body of significant literature stimulated by his work (cf., Goodenough, Chapter 2) and in the words of his peers: "Witkin's concept of field dependence-independence constitutes perhaps the strongest body of evidence available for any trait or style in personality psychology" (Singer, 1984, p. 217); " . . . there seems to be little doubt that Witkin's eventual place in the pantheon of eminent personality researchers is virtually assured . . . what we have witnessed thus far is no less than a prodigious accomplishment" (Kogan, 1980, pp. 595, 598); "Witkin bequeaths us valuable guides for future research along with ample evidence of his rich contribution to psychology" (Korchin, 1982, p. 604).

In identifying the highlights of Witkin's impact on psychology, attention should be given to his focus on individual differences as a route for studying general, functional relations among variables (cf., Goodenough, this volume). Always sensitive to empirical findings rather than dismissing the individual differences that appeared in his studies with Asch on general processes underlying perception of verticality (Asch & Witkin, 1948a, 1948b), Witkin gave those differences special attention; he shaped them with respect to a critical dimension—self-world relationship—and studied their links in very diverse domains, viz., in social interaction, in cultural differences, in psychopathology, in clinical treatment, in neural functioning, and in education. In this way, Witkin forced psychology to recognize that study of individual differences is, like study of general processes, a respectable and fruitful domain for investigation.

One of the most innovative characteristics of Witkin's conceptualization was his effort to draw researchers in psychology to the relationship between part processes and the total organization of personality. In the book, *Personality through Perception* (Witkin et al., 1954), he and his co-workers stressed that perception and (later on) cognitive processes cannot be understood without first describing general properties of cognitive functions with respect to individual differences that are dependent on the total organization of the person. This holistic perspective was articulated by postulating the principles of differentiation and of integration that characterizes the changes in personality during ontogenesis (cf. Werner, 1957).

The concept of differentiation, that is, the notion that properties of a system develop specialized functions, was extensively stressed by Witkin and his co-workers. Its relevance was both theoretically and empirically explored on all levels of functioning: physiological, psychological and sociocultural. In Witkin's last publication (Witkin & Goodenough, 1981), the enormous amount of evidence for all three levels was reviewed and reconceptualized, making available one of the most impressive attempts to theorize on the relationships between these domains, and to provide one of the most powerful, holistically oriented approaches in contemporary psychology to deal with such a diversified body of knowledge.

Witkin's impact on psychology is evident not only from what has been accomplished in the past, but also from how these accomplishments set the stage for future research. We follow Witkin's own suggestion of looking for "lacunae and uncertainties" that open the way for future research as expressed in his own words (Witkin & Goodenough, 1981):

> Though it has changed very much in its lifetime, field-dependence theory is still very much in evolution. We can therefore be quite sure that, just as it has changed in the past, it will appear quite different in the future under the impetus of newly emerging evidence. An evolving theory is inevitably characterized by lacunae and uncertainties. This is surely true of field-dependence theory at this moment. These lacunae and uncertainties in themselves provided an impetus for research which can serve to advance the theory (p. x).

In exemplifying some research directions for the future, we restrict ourselves to five significant problems: the search for underlying processes, the issue of integration at different levels of organization, the conception of field dependence-independence as a bipolar dimension, the notion of mobility-fixity, and the relation between value status of field dependence-independence and culture.

To illustrate the need to search for underlying processes, consider the way in which Witkin and his colleagues studied the relationship between teacher and student. There are multiple ways in which these pairs can be matched and how they could relate to one another. For example, matched pairs (either field dependent or field independent) get along better together if they are working toward a common goal. However, field-independent pairs do not get along very well if they are working toward conflicting goals. A field dependent student learns more if matched with a field-independent teacher who provides the structure that the student needs. Because of this great complexity, it is clearly necessary to carry out studies of processes underlying the outcome of teacher-student relationships, matched or mismatched, with respect to cognitive style.

Whereas the principle of differentiation received great attention and generated much research, the functional relations between the different subsystems and between part of the system and the environment (integration) was formulated in the early stages of the theory but was explored in only a limited set of problems. Psychopathology (See Korchin and also Lewis, this volume) offered clear examples of individuals who presented a high degree of physiological and psychological differentiation but who did not manifest integration between cognition and affection and thereby did not exhibit adequate adjustment to the environment. Thus, integration in psychopathology was tied to effectiveness of adaptation while differentiation was viewed as a person characteristic.

Examination of Witkin's approach shows many examples " . . . which employ integration and other modes of relationship among differentiated parts without recognizing this to be the case" (Wapner, 1984, p. 9). As an example, hierarchic integration may be implicit when there is suppression of visual (bodily) cues for field-independent (dependent) persons and when there is use of particular defences with others subordinated. A systematic reconceptualization, utilizing the coupling of the differentiation concept with integration, might serve to make the theory more heuristic.

To exemplify the potential of such a reconceptualization, let us consider the implications of field dependence theory for research in neurophysiology and cognitive psychology. An important trend in these areas is the discovery of a large number of specialized subsystems. For example, our knowledge of vision includes a variety of cortical areas, each responding to a very selective category of stimuli; similarly, cognitive psychology identifies a very complex map of specific analyzers to account for complex performance, such as decoding verbal material, processing or retrieving visual, tactile, verbal material. This knowledge can be productively confronted with the same question Witkin asked 30 years ago: "How can we explain, given this new information, how individuals differ from one another when confronted with situations which present conflicting information?"

In a classical experiment on field dependence, it was shown that some people (field-dependent) in a tilted room, adjust their subjective vertical, relying on visual rather than proprioceptive cues, while other subjects (field independent) adjusted on the basis of their body position. In general terms, Witkin viewed the individual differences as related to the degree of self/ nonself differentiation: subjects with greater differentiation tend to rely more on internal cues, whereas subjects with less clear boundaries between self and nonself make more use of information in the outside world. Within this framework, two more specific sets of hypotheses can be offered at the neurophysiological level.

The first hypothesis is that each subject has access to visual, proprioceptive, and vestibular information. However, some of these systems are more effective than others and account for the difference in response when the two or more opposite sets of information are in conflict. In addition, the differentiation hypothesis and the developmental state suggest that the balance between these neurophysiological mechanisms should change in a predictable way during the course of ontogenetic development. None of these problems could be raised if the research were guided by information processing oriented approaches.

The second hypothesis implies that each individual at a particular developmental stage has access to all physiological subsystems. These do not differ in their power and thereby do not subordinate one kind of information to another. In this case the explanation calls from some principle of integration between subsystems that accounts for the relative subordination of one process over another when different stimuli need to interact to organize the subject's response. There is need to search for some organizational principle at the neurophysiological level that can account for different ways in which organisms can integrate diverse cues, providing that basic modes of processing are available to all members of the species.

The two alternatives outlined indicate that a more holistic approach can help organize knowledge from different fields and suggest new questions for future investigation. Moreover, the latter hypothesis illustrates the need to explore more vigorously the concept of integration that, though formulated at an early stage in the research program, has not yet been sufficiently elaborated.

The continuing evolution of Witkin's theory, while attempting to react to appropriate criticism of previous formulation and providing a broad "framework for understanding personality and social functioning" (Korchin, Chapter 5), also generated new specific problems to be investigated. Witkin and Goodenough (1981) themselves explicitly indicate some of the directions for future research. In two papers (Witkin and Goodenough, 1981; Witkin, Goodenough and Oltman, 1979) a radical change of differentiation theory was proposed. A hierarchical construct was introduced where "the extent of autonomy of external referents" (to which the label of field dependence-independence has been transferred) was conceived of as a bipolar concept from which subordinate qualities can be identified: restructuring skills and interpersonal competencies.

This new model permits new definitions of field-dependent and field-independent persons, not only as "poor" or "good" with respect to disembedding ability or to the reliance on visual versus bodily information, but as having two sets of orientation. One orientation involves skill in interpersonal relationships; the other involves ability to restructure information coming from the environment. This bipolar (interpersonal skills and restructuring) reconceptualization suggested to the authors that "the very considerable task must first be met of conceptualizing more precisely the nature of interpersonal competencies and devising the tests for their assessment" (Witkin & Goodenough, 1981, p. 54). When this task is achieved, future research can face the problem of testing the new hierarchical ordering postulated by the theory. Witkin and Goodenough (1981) suggest two possible ways of testing. One is a " . . . factor analytic study that yields a pattern of relations among factor scores for the three major constructs: reliance on internal versus external referents; cognitive restructuring skills; and interpersonal competencies" (p. 54).

Witkin and Goodenough (1981) go on: "Another possible approach to checking the hierarchical ordering proposed in our model is through the use of training procedures" (p. 55). The authors suggest that research in psychotherapy would provide a unique situation in which the model could be empirically evaluated. Implicit in the notion of possible modification due to training or psychotherapy is the idea that field dependence is susceptible to change. Early formulations of the theory stressed in particular the stability of style across time and situations. It was directed chiefly toward the identification of modes of functioning characteristic of the person.

Another major shift in reconceptualization had its origins in unpublished research. On the basis of clinical observation, Witkin and Goodenough (1981) now assume that both field-dependent and field-independent people could be either mobile or fixed with respect to cognitive style, that is, whether field dependent or independent. Under various circumstances mobile people could show the characteristics of either cognitive style, that is, interpersonal skills and cognitive restructuring skills. This notion of mobility-fixity makes for an incongruity with earlier conceptualization which stressed the consistency of field dependence-independence. This inconsistency may be the basis for important steps forward in theory and empirical studies. As Witkin and Goodenough (1981) noted, the mobility-fixity notion, coupled with bipolarity of field dependence-independence, suggests the training goal of supplementing existent characteristics of a field-dependent (independent) person with the characteristics of the field-independent (dependent) person. Systematic research evaluating the efficacy of training for social skills and restructuring will have both theoretical and practical value. There is also need for an empirical study of internal (subjective) and external (social, environmental) conditions under which fixity or mobility of each of the styles occur. Furthermore, what conditions make for subordination of a field-dependent to a field-independent cognitive style and vice versa? Systematic analysis of those conditions could both help refine the mobility-fixity concept and define its range of applicability more precisely. It may explain the unaccounted for variance in the high, but not perfect, correlations among diverse variables on different test occasions. The emergence of bidimensionality and the mobility–fixity concept makes clear the need to introduce the concept of integration systematically in accounting for how interpersonal and restructuring skills are related in a given person (cf. Wapner, 1984).

Possibilities for research go beyond analysis of psychological processes and point to relations between psychology and other disciplines, such as cultural anthropology. There is by now a great deal of research that supports the view that field-dependent and field-independent ways of functioning are broadly tuned to the adaptive requirements of different cultural settings. Among subsistence-level groups, people who are extremely field independent often belong to nomadic hunting cultures in which self-reliance is adaptive. Farmers, in contrast, live in larger, sedentary groups that place a premium on interpersonal relationships and have more powerful religious and political authorities that tightly prescribe the individual's role in society. As might be expected on the basis of field-dependence theory, farming people tend to be much more field dependent than hunting people. The differences between cultures in mean levels of field dependence place the bipolar aspects of Witkin's conceptualization in broader perspective. Future research might profitably involve a new approach to the study of individual differences in cognitive styles. It may be true that individuals who are more field independent than their peers are highly valued if they belong to a culture in which field-independent characteristics are particularly adaptive. By the same token, individuals who are more field dependent than their peers may be more highly valued if they belong to a culture in which field-dependent characteristics are particuarly adaptive.

In this epilogue the attempt was made to select for future development a few theoretical issues that have emerged in the fascinating history of field dependence-independence. The discussion was restricted largely to basic research problems. The extraordinary variety of research and its applications discussed in previous chapters speaks for itself of the potential of Witkin's work for unifying knowledge in psychology and its relationships with the biological sciences, the social sciences and education.

REFERENCES

Asch, S. E., & Witkin, H. A. (1948a). Studies in space orientation. I. Perception of the upright with displaced visual fields. *Journal of Experimental Psychology, 38,* 325–337.

Asch, S. E., & Witkin, H. A. (1948b). Studies in space orientation. II. Perception of the upright with displaced visual fields and with the body tilted. *Journal of Environmental Psychology, 38,* 455–477.

Kogan, N. (1980). A style of life, a life of style. *Contemporary Psychology, 25,* 595–598.

Korchin, S. J. (1982). The legacy of H. A. Witkin. *Contemporary Psychology, 27,* 602–604.

Singer, J. L. (1984). *The human personality.* San Diego, CA: Harcourt Brace Jovanovich.

Wapner, S. (1984, November). *A holistic, developmental, systems-oriented analysis of individual differences in cognition.* Paper presented at the International Congress on Individual Differences in Cognition, Catania University, Italy.

Werner, H. (1957). The concept of development from a comparative and organismic point of view. In D. B. Harris (Ed.), *The concept of development: An issue in the study of human behavior.* Minneapolis: University of Minnesota Press.

Witkin, H. A., & Goodenough, D. R. (1981). *Cognitive styles: Essence and origins. Field dependence and field independence.* New York: International Universities Press.

Witkin, H. A., Goodenough, D. R., & Oltman, P. K. (1979). Psychological differentiation: Current status. *Journal of Personality and Social Psychology, 37,* 1127–1145.

Witkin, H. A., Lewis, H. B., Hertzman, M., Machover, K., Meissner, P. B., & Wapner, S. (1954). *Personality through perception.* New York: Harper. (Reprinted 1972, Westport, CT: Greenwood Press.)

Publications of
Herman A. Witkin[1]

BOOKS

Witkin, H. A., Lewis, H. B., Hertzman, M., Machover, K., Meissner, P. B., & Wapner, S. (1972). *Personality through perception: An experimental and clinical study.* Westport, CT: Greenwood Press. (Originally published: New York: Harper & Brothers, 1954.)

Witkin, H. A., Dyk, R. B., Faterson, H. F., Goodenough, D. R., & Karp, S. A. (1974). *Psychological differentiation: Studies of development.* Potomac, MD: Lawrence Erlbaum Associates. (Originally published: New York: Wiley, 1962.) (Trans. into Italian, P. Zoccolotti. (1976). *La differenziazione psicologica.* Roma: Bulzoni.)

Witkin, H. A., & Lewis, H. B. (Eds.) (1967). *Experimental studies of dreaming.* New York: Random House.

Witkin, H. A. (1978). *Cognitive Styles in Personal and Cultural Adaptation.* The 1977 Heinz Werner Lectures. Worcester, MA: Clark University Press.

Witkin, H. A., & Goodenough, D. R. (1981). *Cognitive styles: Essence and origins.* New York: International Universities Press.

JOURNAL ARTICLES & OTHER PUBLICATIONS

Witkin, H. A. (1937). Maze behavior and maze design. *Psychological Bulletin, 34,* 531–532.

Witkin, H. A. (1937). The rat's systematized habits of response in a non-problem situation. *Psychological Bulletin, 34,* 708–709.

Witkin, H. A., & Granich, L. (1937). An application of some principals of maze-mechanics in the planning of a serviceable maze. *Journal of Comparative Psychology, 24,* 523–545.

---

[1]There is available at the Educational Testing Service Archives *A Guide to the Herman A. Witkin Papers* by P. W. Cox and G. D. Saretzky, 1983 (Princeton, NJ: ETS Archives), as well as the papers described.

Witkin, H. A., & Schneirla, T. C. (1937). Initial maze behavior as a function of maze design. *Journal of Comparative Psychology, 23,* 275-304.

Rogosin, H., & Witkin, H. A. (1938). The radio war scare. *The Psychologists League Journal, 2,* 84-86.

Witkin, H. A. (1938). "Hypotheses" in rats: A critique. *Psychological Bulletin, 35,* 638.

Witkin, H. A. (1939). Abnormal behavior in animals. *The Psychologists League Journal, 3,* 75-83.

Witkin, H. A. (1940). "Hypotheses" in rats: An experimental critique: I. The genesis of systematic behavior in linear situations. *Journal of Comparative Psychology, 30,* 457-482.

Witkin, H. A. (1941). "Hypotheses" in rats: An experimental critique: II. The displacement of responses and behavior variability in linear situations. *Journal of Comparative Psychology, 31,* 303-336.

Witkin, H. A. (1942). "Hypotheses" in rats: An experimental critique: III. Summary evaluation of the hypotheses concept. *Psychological Review, 49,* 541-568.

Witkin, H. A. (1942). Restriction as a factor in adjustment to conflict situations. *Journal of Comparative Psychology, 33,* 41-74.

Witkin, H. A. (1946). Studies in geographic orientation. *Year Book of the American Philosophical Society,* 152-155.

Asch, S. E., & Witkin, H. A. (1948). Studies in space orientation: I. Perception of the upright with displaced visual fields. *Journal of Experimental Psychology, 38,* 325-337.

Asch, S. E., & Witkin, H. A. (1948). Studies in space orientation: II. Perception of the upright with displaced visual fields and with body tilted. *Journal of Experimental Psychology, 38,* 455-477.

Witkin, H. A. (1948). *The effect of training and of structural aids on performance in three tests of space orientation.* (Report No. 80). Washington, D.C.: Civil Aeronautics Administration, Division of Research.

Witkin, H. A., & Asch, S. E. (1948). Studies in space orientation: III. Perception of the upright in the absence of a visual field. *Journal of Experimental Psychology, 38,* 603-614.

Witkin, H. A., & Asch, S. E. (1948). Studies in space orientation: IV. Further experience on perception of the upright with displaced visual fields. *Journal of Experimental Psychology, 38,* 762-782.

Witkin, H. A. (1949, Dec.). Orientation in space. *Research Reviews,* 1-7.

Witkin, H. A. (1949). Perception of body position and of the position of the visual field. *Psychological Monographs: General and Applied, 63,* 1-46. (Whole No. 302)

Witkin, H. A. (1949). Sex differences in perception. *Transactions of the New York Academy of Sciences,* Series II, *12,* No. 1, 22-26.

Witkin, H. A. (1949). The nature and importance of individual differences in perception. *Journal of Personality, 18,* 145-170.

Wapner, S., & Witkin, H. A. (1950). The role of visual factors in the maintenance of body balance. *American Journal of Psychology, LXIII,* 385-408.

Witkin, H. A. (1950). Individual differences in ease of perception of embedded figures. *Journal of Personality, 19,* 1-15.

Witkin, H. A. (1950, October). *Individual differences in mode of space orientation.* Paper presented at a symposium on Psychophysiological Factors in Spatial Orientation at the meeting of the Naval Research Advisory Panel in Psychophysiology, U.S. Naval School of Aviation Medicine, Pensacola, FL. (Report No. MAVEXOS P-966). Washington, D.C.: Office of Naval Research.

Witkin, H. A. (1950). Perception of the upright when the direction of the force acting on the body is changed. *Journal of Experimental Psychology, 40,* 93-106.

Witkin, H. A., & Wapner, S. (1950). Visual factors in the maintenance of upright posture. *American Journal of Psychology, LXIII,* 31-50.

Witkin, H. A. (1952). Further studies of perception of the upright when the direction of the force acting on the body is changed. *Journal of Experimental Psychology, 43,* 9–20.

Witkin, H. A., Wapner, S., & Leventhal, T. (1952). Sound localization with conflicting visual and auditory cues. *Journal of Experimental Psychology, 43,* 58–67.

Witkin, H. A. (1953). Comment on "The role of instruction in experimental space orientation." *Journal of Experimental Psychology, 46,* 135–136.

Witkin, H. A. (1959). The perception of the upright. *Scientific American, 200,* 50–56.

Witkin, H. A., Karp, S. A., & Goodenough, D. R. (1959). Dependence in Alocholics. *Quarterly Journal of Studies on Alcohol, 20,* 493–504.

Witkin, H. A. (1960). "Embedded figures and personality:" A reply. *Perceptual and Motor Skills, 11,* 15–20.

Witkin, H. A. (1960). Psychological self-consistency. *Transactions of the New York Academy of Sciences, 22,* 541–545.

Witkin, H. A. (1961). Cognitive development and the growth of personality. *Acta Psychologica, 18,* 245–257.

Witkin, H. A. (1962). The problem of individuality in development. In S. Wapner & B. Kaplan (Eds.), *Perspectives in psychological theory* (pp. 335–361). New York: International Universities Press.

Bertini, M., Lewis, H. B., & Witkin, H. A. (1964). Some preliminary observations with an experimental procedure for the study of hypnagogic and related phenomena. *Archivio di Psicologia, Neurologia e Psichiatra, 25,* 493–534.

Witkin, H. A. (1964). Origins of cognitive style. In C. Sheerer (Ed.), *Cognition: Theory, research, promise* (pp. 172–205). New York: Harper & Row.

Witkin, H. A. (1964). Uses of the centrifuge in studies of the orientation of space. *American Journal of Psychology, 77,* 499–501.

Dyk, R. B., & Witkin, H. A. (1965). Family experiences related to the development of differentiation in children. *Child Development, 30,* 21–55.

Karp, S. A., Witkin, H. A., & Goodenough, D. R. (1965). Alcoholism and psychological differentiation: Effect of achievement of sobriety on field dependence. *Quarterly Journal of Studies on Alcohol, 26,* 580–585.

Karp, S. A., Witkin, H. A., & Goodenough, D. R. (1965). Alcoholism and psychological differentiation: Effect of alcohol on field dependence. *Journal of Abnormal Psychology, 70,* 262–265.

Rosenblum, L. A., Witkin, H. A., Kaufman, I. C., & Brosgole, L. (1965). Perceptual disembedding in monekys: Note on method and preliminary findings. *Perceptual and Motor Skills, 20,* 729–736.

Witkin, H. A. (1965). Development of body concept and psychological differentiation. In S. Wapner & Werner (Eds.), *The Body Percept* (pp. 26–48). New York: Random House.

Witkin, H. A. (1965). Heinz Werner: 1890–1964. *Child Development, 30,* 308–328.

Witkin, H. A. (1965). Psychological differentiation and forms of pathology. *Journal of Abnormal Psychology, 1965, 70,* 317–336. (Reproduced in: *Bulletin de L'association Internationale de Psychologie Appliquée, 1965, 14,* 48–67. *Przeglad Psychologiczny, 1965, 16,* 75–104. *Psyche: Zeitschrift fur Psychoanalyse und Ihre Anwendungen, 1973, 27,* 555–593. *Revista di Psycologia General y Aplicada, 1964, 19,* 945–966.)

Witkin, H. A. (1965). Some implications of research on cognitive style for problems of education. *Archivio di Psicologia, Neurologia e Psichiatria, 26,* 27–55. (Originally a paper presented at the Institute on the Social and Emotional Problems of the Child in the Regular Classroom, University of Rochester (1962, October). Reproduced in: *Archivio di Psicologia, Neurologia e Psichiatria, 1966, 27,* 369–396. M. G. and G. B. Gottsegen (Eds.), *Professional School Psychology,* Vol. III. New York: Grune & Stratton, 1969.

Witkin, H. A., & Lewis, H. B. (1965). The relation of experimentally induced presleep experiences to dreams. *Journal of the American Psychoanalytic Association, 13,* 819-849.

Witkin, H. A., Faterson, H. F., Goodenough, D. R., & Birnbaum, J. (1966). Cognitive patterning in mildly retarded boys. *Child Development, 37,* 301-316.

Witkin, H. A. (1967). A cognitive style approach to cross-cultural research. *International Journal of Psychology, 2,* 233-250.

Witkin, H. A., Goodenough, D. R., & Karp, S. A. (1967). Stability of cognitive style from childhood to young adulthood. *Journal of Personality and Social Psychology, 7,* 291-300.

Witkin, H. A., & Lewis, H. B. (1967). Presleep experiences and dreams. In H. A. Witkin & H. B. Lewis (Eds.), *Experimental Studies of Dreaming* (pp. 148-202). New York: Random House.

Witkin, H. A., & Oltman, P. K. (1967). Cognitive style. *International Journal of Neurology, 6,* 119-137.

Witkin, H. A., Birnbaum, J., Lononaco, S., Lehr, S., & Herman, J. L. (1968). Cognitive patterning in congenitally totally blind children. *Child Development, 39,* 767-786.

Witkin, H. A., Lewis, H. B., & Weil, E. (1968). Affective reactions and patient-therapist interactions among more differentiated and less differentiated patients early in therapy. *Journal of Nervous and Mental Disease, 146,* 193-208.

Witkin, H. A. (1969). Influencing dream content. In M. Kramer (Ed.), *Dream Psychology and the New Biology of Dreaming* (pp. 285-359). Springfield, Ill.: Charles C. Thomas.

Witkin, H. A. (1969). Presleep experiences and dreams. In J. Fisher & L. Bregar (Eds.), *The Meaning of Dreams: Recent Insights From the Laboratory.* California Mental Health Research Symposium, No. *3,* 1-37.

Witkin, H. A. (1969). Social influences in the development of cognitive style. In D. A. Goslin (Ed.), *Handbook of socialization theory and research* (pp. 687-706). New York: Rand, McNally.

Faterson, H. F., & Witkin, H. A. (1970). Longitudinal study of development of the body concept. *Developmental Psychology, 2,* 429-438.

Witkin, H. A. (1970). Individual differences in dreaming. In E. Hartmann (Ed.), *Sleep and dreaming.* Boston: Little Brown. (Also cited as *International Psychiatry Clinics,* 1970, *7,* No. 2, 153-164.)

Witkin, H. A., Birnbaum, J., Lononaco, S., Lehr, S., & Herman, J. L. (1970). Cognitive patterning in congenitally totally blind children. In L. R. Aronson, E. Tobach, J. S. Rosenblatt, & D. S. Lehrman (Eds.), *Development and evolution of behavior,* Vol. 1, Essays in Memory of T. C. Schneirla. San Francisco: W. H. Freeman.

Witkin, H. A. (1971). Foreword to *Shame and guilt in neuroses,* by Helen Block Lewis. New York: International Universities Press.

Witkin, H. A., Oltman, P. K., Chase, J. B., & Friedman, F. (1971). Cognitive patterning in the blind. I J. Hellmuth (Ed.), *Cognitive studies,* Vol. 2: *Deficits in cognition.* New York: Brunner, Mazel.

Freedman, M., O'Hanlon, J., Oltman, P. K., & Witkin, H. A. (1972). The imprint of psychological differentiation on kinetic behavior in varying communicative contexts. *Journal of Abnormal Psychology, 79,* 239-258.

Witkin, H. A., Mensh, I. N., & Cates, J. (1972). Psychologists in medical schools. *American Psychologist, 27,* 434-440.

Witkin, H. A. (1973). *The role of cognitive style in academic performance and in teacher-student relations.* Paper presented at a symposium on "Cognitive Styles, Creativity and Higher Education," sponsored by the Graduate Record Examination Board, Montreal, Canada. Princeton, N.J.: Educational Testing Service, Research Bulletin 73-11.

Witkin, H. A., Oltman, P. K., Cox, P. W., Ehrlichman, E., Hamm, R. M., & Ringler, R. W. (1973). *Field-dependence-independence and Psychological Differentiation: A Bibliography Through 1972 With Index.* Princeton, N.J.: Educational Testing Service, Research Bulletin 73-62.

Goodenough, D. R., Witkin, H. A., Lewis, H. B., Komlack, D., & Cohen, H. (1974). Regression, interferences and field dependence as factors in dream forgetting. *Journal of Abnormal Psychology, 83,* No. 1, 32–44. (Also ETS Research Bulletin 73-58, 1973)

Witkin, H. A. (1974). A cognitive-style perspective on evaluation and guidance. From *Proceedings of the 1973 Invitational Conference on Testing Problems—Measurement for self-understanding and personal development.* Princeton, N.J.: Educational Testing Service, 21–27.

Witkin, H. A. (1974, December). Educational implications of cognitive style. *Proceedings of the Fourteenth Annual Meeting of the Council of Graduate Schools.* Phoenix, Arizona.

Witkin, H. A., Cox, P. W., Friedman, F., Hrishikesan, A. G., & Siegel, K. N. (1974). *Field-dependence-independence and Psychological Differentiation. A Bibliography With Index. Supplement No. 1.* Princeton, N.J.: Educational Testing Service, Research Bulleton 74-42.

Witkin, H. A., Price-Williams, D., Bertini, M., Christiansen, B., Oltman, P. K., Ramirez, M., & van Meel, J. (1974). Social Conformity and psychological differentiation. *International Journal of Psychology, 9,* 11–29. (Also ETS Research Bulletin 73-63, 1973)

Cohen, H. D., Goodenough, D. R., Witkin, H. A., Oltman, P., Gould, H., & Shulman, E. (1975). The effects of stress on components of the respiration cycle. *Psychophysiology, 12,* 377–380.

Goodenough, D. R., Witkin, H. A., Koulack, D., & Cohen, H. (1975). The effects of stress films on dream affect and on respiration and eye-movement activity during rapid-eye-movement sleep. *Psychophysiology, 12,* 313–320.

Oltman, P. K., Goodenough, D. R., Witkin, H. A., Freedman, N., & Friedman, F. (1975). Psychological differentiation as a factor in conflict resolution. *Journal of Personality & Social Psychology, 32,* 730–736. (Also ETS Research Bulletin 74-27, 1974)

Witkin, H. A., & Berry, J. W. (1975). Psychological differentiation in cross-cultural perspective. *Journal of Cross-Cultural Psychology, 3,* (1), 4–87. (Also ETS Research Bulletin 75-4, 1975)

Witkin, H. A., & Cox, P. W. (1975). Cognitive styles: New tool for career guidance? *ETS Findings, 2,* 1–4.

Witkin, H. A. (1976). Cognitive style in academic performance and in teacher-student relations. In S. Messick & Associates (Eds.), *Individuality in Learning: Implications of Cognitive Styles and Creativity in Human Development.* San Francisco: Jossey-Bass.

Witkin, H. A. (1976). *Foreword to Human Ecology and Cognitive Style: Comparative Studies in Cultural and Psychological Adaptation,* by John W. Berry. New York: Wiley.

Witkin, H. A., Cox, P. W., & Friedman, F. (1976). *Field-dependence-independence and Psychological Differentiation: A Bibliography With Index. Supplement No. 2.* Princeton, NJ: Educational Testing Service, Research Bulletin 76-28.

Witkin, H. A., Mednick, S. A., Schulsinger, F., Bakkestrom, E., Christiansen, K. O., Goodenough, D. R., Hirschhorn, K., Lundsteen, C., Owen, D. R., Philip, J., Rubin, D. B., & Stocking, M. (1976). Criminality in XYY and XXY men. *Science, 193,* 547–555.

Goodenough, D. R., Gandini, E., Olkin, I., Pizzamiglio, L., Thayer, D., & Witkin, H. A. (1977). A study of X-chromosome linkage with field-dependence and spatial-visualization. *Journal of Behavioral Genetics, 7,* 373–387.

Goodenough, D. R., & Witkin, H. A. (1977). *Origins of the Field-dependent and Field-independent Cognitive Styles.* Princeton, NJ: Educational Testing Service, Research Bulletin 77-9.

Witkin, H. A. (1977). Cognitive styles in the educational setting. *New York University Education Quarterly, 8,* 14–20.

Witkin, H. A. (1977). Cross-cultural perspectives on psychological differentiation in children and their implications for education. In Y. Poortinga (Ed.), *Basic problems in cross-cultural psychology.* Amsterdam: Swets & Zeitlinger.

Witkin, H. A. (1977). Theory in cross-cultural research: Its uses and risks. In Y. Poortinga (Ed.), *Basic problems in cross-cultural psychology.* Amsterdam: Swets & Zeitlinger.

Witkin, H. A., & Goodenough, D. R. (1977). Field dependence and interpersonal behavior. *Psychological Bulletin, 84,* 661–689. (Also ETS Research Bulletin 76-12, 1976)

Witkin, H. A., & Goodenough, D. R. (1977). *Field Dependence Revisited.* Princeton, NJ: Educational Testing Service, Research Bulletin 77-16. (Supercedes ETS RB 76-39)

Witkin, H. A., Goodenough, D. R., & Hirschhorn, K. (1977). XYY Men: Are they criminally aggressive? *The Sciences, 17,* 10–13.

Witkin, H. A., Moore, C. A., Goodenough, D. R., & Cox, P. W. (1977). Field-dependent and field-independent cognitive styles and their educational implications. *Reviews of Educational Research, 47,* 1–64. (Reproduced in *L'Orientation Scolaire et Professionelle,* 1978, *7,* 299–349.) (Also ETS Research Bulletin 75-24, 1975)

Witkin, H. A., Moore, C. A., Oltman, P. K., Goodenough, D. R., Friedman, F., Owen, D. R., & Raskin, E. (1977). The role of the field-dependent and field-independent cognitive styles in academic evolution: A longitudinal study. *Journal of Educational Psychology, 69,* 197–211. (Also ETS Research Bulletin 76-35, 1976. Longer version: Graduate Record Examinations Board Research Report No. 76-10R. Reprint #73)

Cox, P. W., & Witkin, H. A. (1978). *Field-dependence-independence and Psychological Differentiation: A Bibliography With Index. Supplement No. 3.* Princeton, NJ: Educational Testing Service, Research Bulletin 78-8.

Dasen, P. R., Berry, J. W., & Witkin, H. A. (1979). The use of development theories cross-culturally. In H. Eckensberger, W. J. Lonner, & Y. H. Poortinga (Eds.), *Cross-cultural Contributions to Psychology.* Amsterdam: Swets & Zeitlinger.

Goodenough, D. R., Oltman, P. K., Friedman, F., Moore, C. A., Witkin, H. A., Owen, D., & Raskin, E. (1979). Cognitive styles in the development of medical careers. *Journal of Vocational Behavior, 14,* 341–351. (Also ETS Research Bulletin 77-21, 1977)

Witkin, H. A. (1979). Estilos cognoscitivos a traves de las culturas. [Cognitive styles across cultures.] In G. E. Finley & G. Marin (Eds.), *Avances en psicologia contemporanea.* Mexico City: Trillas.

Witkin, H. A. (1979). Socialization, culture and ecology in the development of group and sex differences in cognitive style. *Human Development, 22,* 358–372.

Witkin, H. A., Goodenough, D. R., & Oltman, P. K. (1979). Psychological differentiation: Current status. *Journal of Personality and Social Psychology, 37,* 1127–1145. (Also ETS Research Bulletin 77-17, 1977)

Witkin, H. A., & Goodenough, D. R. (1981). *Cognitive styles: Essence and origins. Field dependence and field independence.* New York: International Universities Press.

Author Index

Subject Index